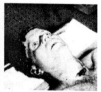

Powers Behind JFK Assassination
By Randolph Jason Polasek

For orders with author's signature, buy at:
www.powersbehindjfkassassination.com
ISBN 978-1-4357-4253-6
For online & retail orders, buy at:
Lulu.com

Dedicated to:

To all those baby boomers, as children,
suffered through the trying time of this horrific event,
and have waited for 45 years to know the truth,
hopefully you will find peace in reading this and
closure to a tragic assassination we both lived through.

1st Edition 2008
All copyrights reserved 2008
Lulu Publisher
Lulu.com
ISBN 978-1-4357-4253-6

Contents

Thank You!

To all those who have touched me in a positive way, I thank you.
Fore you in-part are the reason I am the way I am, for the better, I pray.
Fore those I've touched,
I pray my effect on your life made it more pleasant.
To all those who have touched me in a harmful, negative way,
I forgive you.

To those Oakland University genius-students in Rochester, Michigan,
that were at the Wilson Library on Saturdays in the mid-1960s,
when I spent hours reading volumes of the Warren Report,
I thank you for your kindness towards a young teenager that I was back then;
especially to the brunette that brought me an ice cold cola one day.

To the many investigative writers, I thank you for your effort
in your search for the truth.
I hope this book answers some of your questions.

To the tens of thousands, for half a century that spoke out in protest of our government locking away the truth of the assassination and the names of characters related to it, I applaud your effort, and I thank you.

I hope someday my grandchildren, in their old age,
will be the first generation that finally are allowed
to see all of the evidence, without blacked out sections
that have covered up all of the players, directly or indirectly,
involved in these crimes of assassination and cover up.

Preface

Since the time I seen Lee Oswald shot down on live TV at the tender age of twelve years, his cold blooded murder while police detectives and police officers stood by, was the beginning of my suspicion that there is more going on with Oswald and President Kennedy's Assassination than meets the eye. Like millions of other Americans, there was something suspiciously missing to the tragic event of an accused assassin not allowed to tell his side of the story in court while police and the news media all but judged him guilty "beyond any reason for doubt."

Shortly after the Warren Commission Report was made public, I as a teenager had the opportunity to read the volumes of the Report. For hours I'd spend reading page after page of eyewitness testimony and description after description of material evidence, but always came away with an empty feeling; as if there was something missing.

For years after, I watched TV Specials and documentaries tear apart the creatibility of the Warren Report until I, much like most people, judged the Report as fiction. Many books have come out the past forty-five years, each with their theory of who were the shooters of President Kennedy. Anyone and everyone that had came in contact with the "accused" assassin, Lee Oswald, had something to do with President Kennedy's Assassination; that is, if one would believe all the conspiracy theories.

Years ago I stopped being led astray by such theories and began reading up on the history of the characters involved, American history, President Kennedy's Administration and the creation and history of the United States Central Banking Systems and its owners.

The journey my book will take you on is as historical and educational as intriguing. I won't waste your time with theories on assassins, since they were only hired guns to the Assassination. What I will show you is a pattern of violent behavior by a group of people that did whatever means necessary to keep the power that controlling America's currency. This power has been handed down within the same families for generations. After you carefully read to understand the pattern of these powerful and wealthy people, will you truly understand the ***Powers Behind JFK Assassination*** and those I name with evidence to their direct or indirect involvement to **President Kennedy's Assassination and cover up...** *"ENJOY your journey!"*

For over a century, a war has been going on!

Between the capitalists and government control

Corporations want to run their Empire without regulations
while governmental regulations
protect citizens from corporate unending GREED!

Without
regulations
& oversight,
polluting
corporations
aren't held
accountable
while
pollution
of our air
and deminishing
water supplies CONTINUES!

Deregulating the media enabled corporations to avoid taxes by buying their competition and monopolizing their markets while controlling and limiting the news they report.

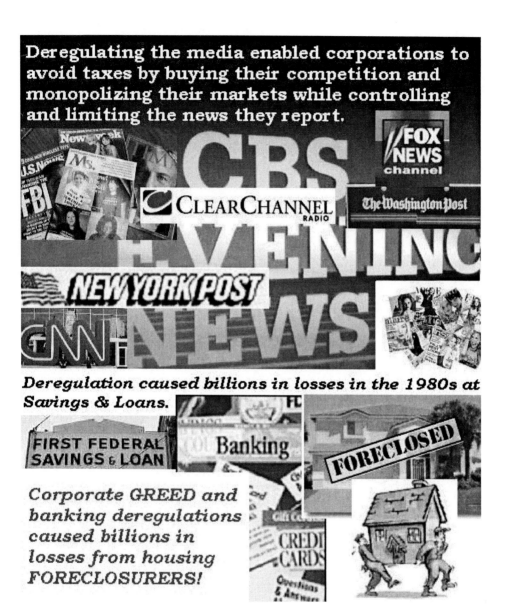

Deregulation caused billions in losses in the 1980s at Savings & Loans.

Corporate GREED and banking deregulations caused billions in losses from housing FORECLOSURERS!

Corporations

Big Business want only two things... profits and more PROFITS!

They DEMAND Control!

And Will Do Anything To Stay In Control!

Chapter I
The "Business Plot" to overthrow President Roosevelt

Major General Smedley Butler in 1933 was the most decorated Marine in United States history. He testified before the McCormick-Dickstein Committee in 1934, that he was approached the previous year by a group of men representing some of the most powerful and wealthy businessmen including Du Pont, Rockefeller, Ford, Bush, Walker, Harriman, Goodyear and J.P. Morgan. Their interest was in him to lead the military to overthrow the Roosevelt Administration and replace it with a pro-big business, fascist government. Although

Smedley Butler   the Committee's final report verified a plot was well past the the planning stage, no action was taken against anyone and the subject was dropped.

J. P. Morgan   John D. Rockefeller Sr. & Jr.   P. S. Du Pont   Rothschilds

J.P. Morgan was a central figure in the plot to overthrow President Roosevelt, was an early "puppet" to the Rothschilds in Great Britain and later a "puppet master" to many when he held over 160 industrial, financial and banking concerns after moving to U.S.

John D. Rockefeller would be considered "the richest man in the world" after developing Standard Oil to supply over 91% of the nation's oil and gasoline. He was known as a ruthless businessman. The Rockefeller based company Standard Oil's marriage with IG Farben, the company which manufactured Zyklon B,(poison gas) for the Nazi Party, demonstrated a lack of ethics towards its business practices. Today, the Rockefellers own a substantial amount of stock in ExxonMobil.

Pierre S. DuPont served as President and on the Board of Directors of Du Pont Company. He also served as Chairman and President of General Motors.

Rothschild Family was one of the largest and most powerful banking institution throughout Europe since the mid-1700s and was a major stockholder in the Central Bank of England, the early United States Central Banks and today's Federal Reserve

9

Brown Brothers Harriman and Company

W. Averall Harriman* Robert Lovett* George H. Walker*   Prescott S. Bush*
Founding partners not pictured: E. Roland Harriman*, Knight Woolley*, Moreau
Delano, Thatcher Brown, Louis Curtis*, Granger Costikyan* and Ray Morris*.
*Denotes members of SKULL & BONES SECRET SOCIETY

Brown Brothers Harriman today is the oldest and largest privately owned banking partnership in the United States and are the lone trustee for Skull & Bone's "Russell Trust Association." Founded in 1931, some of the firm's members were silent partners in the "Business Plot" to overthrow President Roosevelt. They were the Wall Street connection for the Nazis. Four of their many subsidiary companies they controlled were seized by the United State Government under the "Trading with the enemy Act." Union Bank of New York was contrived by E. Rowland Harriman and Prescott Bush to do business with the German industrial empire of Fritz Thyssen, who financed Hitler and the Nazis. Although Prescott owned only 1 of 4,000 shares, he was given 3,991 voting shares to run the Bank as he saw fit; most of which shares were owned by Thyssen. Union Bank laundered German money for the Nazis in exchange for U.S. Treasury Bonds, gold, steel, coal and arms. Also controlled by Brown Brothers Harriman and seized by the government were Holland-American Trading, Seamless Steel and Silesian-American Corporations. International attorney and OSS Director in Berlin, Allen Dulles, misdirected investigations into them after World War II and it wasn't until decades later that their entire involvement with Thyssen and the Nazis would be exposed. (Later explained in detail in Chapter 9, *"A Tale of Two Powerful Political Families."*)

In 1932, the then Governor of New York, Franklin D. Roosevelt, with the backing of newspaper magnate William Randolph Hearst, Irish leader Joseph P. Kennedy and California leader William G. McAdoo upset incumbent President Hoover. Texas leader, John Nance Garner, would switch democratic alliances only after offered to be the vice-president candidate. The country was in the "Great Depression" that would spread worldwide and Roosevelt believed the Federal Reserve's irresponsible handling of the government's money was responsible. What should have been sporadic cash shortages at smaller local banks, turned into an epidemic of runs on the bank's cash through out the country after word got out the Federal Reserve was unable to cover cash flow shortages; a service the Federal Reserve Central Banking System was set up to do.

Congressman MacFadden would later point out in 1933, that the owners of the privately owner Federal Reserve had abused their power by using money intended on preventing "banking panics" that caused "runs on local bank's cash flow" for their own industrial and financial empires. They would secure huge loans for their own financial institutions to make international loans to exploit a country's government, businesses and wealthy individuals. Their goal was to entice foreigners with huge amounts of loans to get them deep into debt, then get them to over extend themselves with more loans until they were forced into selling some of their assets, which the owners of the Federal Reserve's industrial and/or financial institutions would gladly buy for a price far less than its value. They were also using these loans to gain favor from foreign governments and companies for their own empire, at the expense of American citizens and their banks that was counting on the Federal Reserve to prevent "cash flow shortages" with added cash.

President-elect Roosevelt was on to the owners of the Federal Reserve way of doing business and expressed interest in looking into ending their reign of printing, distributing and rating the United States currency.

On February 15th, 1933, only 17 days before Roosevelt's inauguration, a supposing "lone gunman" fired five shots at the President-elect, but hitting the Mayor of Chicago, Anton Cermack. Police reports said six people were shot and six bullets recovered from a gun able to hold only five bullets. Assassin Giuseppi Zangara pleaded guilty to firing three times before he was restrained by the crowd. Mayor Cermack would die of his wounds in less than three weeks. Zangara was sentenced to death on March 20th of 1933 and his execution was carried out ten days later.

President Roosevelt during his twelve years of office had a change of heart in taking on the powers behind the Federal Reserve privately owned Central Banking System. It is not clear why Roosevelt backed away from ending the unconstitutional reign over the printing, distribution and regulating of the United States currency. Some believe it was the President's need of loans from the Federal Reserve for his "back to work" programs. Others said it was out of fear from a combination of the assassination attempt on his life and the Business Plot to overthrow him from office.

President Kennedy 30 years later in 1963 would challenge the powerful bankers that owned the Federal Reserve with Executive Order #11110. The Order would of put the Federal Reserve out of business within six years and give back the constitutional right and duty to the U.S. Treasury to print, distribute and regulate America's currency. But Kennedy's plan to end the irresponsible and ruthless reign of the privately owned Federal Reserve and eliminate the national debt ended only four months after signing Executive Order #11110 by his assassination.

Chapter II
History of United States Banking

The **House of Rothschild** banking family helped finance America's central banking systems, whose history is filled with battles between foreign interference, capitalist's elite, farmers and the common depositor.

"Give me the power to issue a nation's money, and I care not who writes the laws."

- Mayer A. Rothschild

Mayer A. Rothschild, 1744-1812. Born in Germany as Mayer Amschel Bauer, he was founder of the Rothschild Banking Empire that would become one of the most successful family businesses in history. Mayer was known to many as the "founding father to international finance." Rothschild first developed a finance house in Frankfurt, Germany, and then sent 4 of his 5 sons to European cities to set up banking institutions while his eldest son, Mayer Jr., stayed at home to run the Frankfurt office.

Mayer Amschel Rothschild's 5 Sons

| Salomon Mayer 1774-1855 *Rothschild Family Banking of Austria* Lost buildings to Nazis and forced to sell to Merck, Finck Company. | Nathan Mayer 1777-1836 *Rothschild Family Banking of England* Backed Bank of England Rockefeller J.P. Morgan Harriman U.S. Federal Reserve | Amschel Mayer 1773-1855 *Rothschild Family Banking of Germany* With no heirs closed in 1901 Backed 1st & 2nd Bank of the United States | Calman Mayer 1788-1855 *Rothschild Family Banking of Italy* Unification of Italy in 1861 closed. | James Mayer 1792-1868 *Rothschild Family Banking of France* In 2005 merged with England's House. Bank of North America |

United States Banking

Bank of North America   First Bank of United States   Second Bank of United States

Bank of North America

Bank of North America opened on January 7th, 1782 in Philadelphia, Pennsylvania and was under the direction of North America's Finance Minister Robert Morris.

"It was impossible that the business of finance could be ably conducted by a body of men however well composed or well intentioned. Order in the future management of our moneyed concerns, a strict regard to the performance of public engagement, and of course the restoration of public credit maybe reasonably and confidently expected from Robert Morris' administration if he is furnished with materials upon which to operate— that is, if the Federal Government can acquire funds as the basis of his arrangements." - Alexander Hamilton

Robert Morris, from loans by the Netherlands, France and Rothschild Banking, deposited large sums of gold, silver and "bill of exchange" to back the Bank's new paper currency. He also managed to meet the interest rate on the debt, estimated at thirty million dollars. The Bank of North America along with the First Bank of the United States and The Bank of New York obtained the first shares in the New York Stock Exchange.

George Washington to James Madison
"No generation has the right to contract debts greater than can be paid off during the the course of their exsistence."

"History records that the Money Changers have used every form of abuse, intrigue, deceit and violent means possible to maintain their control over governments by controlling money and their issuance." - James Madison

13

"I sincerely believe that banking institutions are more dangerous to our liberties than standing armies. Already they have raised up a money aristocracy that has set the government at defiance. The issuing power should be taken from the banks and restored to the people to whom it properly belongs. –Thomas Jefferson

First Bank of the United States

The First Bank of the United States was chartered by Congress on February 25th, 1791. As a central bank for the newly formed United States, it would put out a uniform currency for all 13 colonies, give credit within the country and overseas. They were forbidden to buy government bonds, occur debt and would have a mandatory rotation of directors. Their charter would be for 20 years, 1791 to 1811, after which a renewal by Congress is needed for the Bank to stay in business. Overseas interests were allowed to buy stock, but not allowed to vote.

"I place the economy among the first and most important virtues and debt as the greatest of dangers to be feared." Thomas Jefferson

Secretary of State Thomas Jefferson and Representative James Madison, as well as most members from southern states in both the Senate and House, were against a central bank or mint. They believed such an institution controlling currency and loans would favor the northern commercial businesses over the southern agricultural interests, which did turn out to be the case. It was left up to President Washington to decide, who was hesitant of signing any banking bill. Jefferson and Madison believed a central bank of private ownership by fellow countrymen and foreigners was unconstitutional and feverously argued against any privately owned central banking bill. Just as passionately, Secretary of the Treasury Alexander Hamilton and his northern congressmen, debated for the bill. On April 25th, 1791 Washington signed a banking bill into law and the central bank became chartered for twenty years.

Thomas Jefferson despised the central banking system as an "un-Godly tool for speculation, manipulation and corruption." After being elected as President in 1801, by 1804 Jefferson had withdrawn all of the government's money from the central bank, thus crippling its existence. The First Bank of the United States' charter expired in 1811, as did the central bank in 1815.

"If the American people ever allow private banks to control the issue of their money, first by inflation, then by deflation, the banks and corporations that will growup around them, will deprive the people of their property until their children wake up homeless on their continent their fathers conquered." - Thomas Jefferson

Second Bank of the United States

Chartered in 1816, patterned after the "First Bank of the United States," President Madison reluctantly signed the central banking bill out of desperation after experiencing how difficult it was for the government to raise currency during the 1812 War. The bank would again, issue currency; handle the government's fiscal affairs and handout loans to fund the expanding new frontier.

With the Napoleonic Wars over by 1816 and much of Western Europe's agriculture in shambles, United States farming products and their land suddenly became in great demand, especially in the south.

The Second Bank of the United States aided to the land boom by allowing loans for land to anyone on request. Land prices doubled and sometimes tripled. But while profits were soaring for many farmers, land speculators for profit only, over extended themselves while the Bank's fraud and corruption went unnoticed. The United States Government had borrowed a big chunk of the Bank's reserves to pay debts from the 1812 War. The Bank also made uneducated loans to desperate European governments and businesses who would sign anything just to get their hands on sound currency while the Bank falsely foresaw unending riches coming to them from their loans with interest, in so much that they over extended themselves.

By 1818, the first economic boom for United States goods, land and currency was declining while European governments and businesses were recovering and no longer desperate for U.S. goods, as well as their loans. Due to the Second Bank of the United States irresponsible massive over extension of loans in foreign lands, they were forced to cut back on homeland loans and begin calling in loans. To the land speculators who were betting on their land increasing in value, they also were over extended and forced to default on their loans. European governments and businesses, more experienced on international financial laws, also began defaulting on their loans. The "1819 Panic" had

15

begun with "runs on banks" for cash by depositors causing bank closings throughout the United States. By 1824, the worst of the Bank's crisis was over and recovery was beginning.

"...beyond question, this great and powerful institution have been actively engaged in attempting to influence the election of public officers with its money."

- President Andrew Jackson

In 1828, Andrew Jackson was elected President, and like President Jefferson, he was against the United States having a privately owned central banking system. President Jackson pulled out the government's money from the Bank in 1836, causing the "1837 Panic," and all but dooming the Bank's future. England's reaction to Jackson was to suspend all American paper money, causing the United States to fall into a Depression. The Second Bank of the United States was not re-chartered in 1838, closing twenty-eight branches while leaving banking to states to regulate and control their currency. In 1841, the Second Bank of the United States went bankrupt, leaving stockholders, foreign and domestic, empty handed with worthless dollars.

Drawing of Richard Lawrence's attempted assassination of Pres. Jackson.

On January 30, 1835, at the Capitol Building, Richard Lawrence aimed two flintlock pistols at President Jackson, but both pistols misfired. Lawrence was apprehended after Jackson beat him with his cane, found not guilty of attempted murder by reason of insanity and confined to a mental institution until his death in 1861.

Free Banking Era 1837-1862

With the elimination of the national central banking system, when there were only state chartered banks, in came the "Free Banking Era." Banks could issue bank notes against their species of gold and silver coins. The states regulated their reserve requirements, interest rates for loans and deposits. State banks turned out to be very unstable with half the banks failing. On an average, the state banks stayed in business only five years. In New York, to assure depositors that their money was safe, New York Safety Fund was created as deposit insurance for member banks. In Boston, Suffolk Bank guaranteed bank notes and acted as a private bank note clearinghouse.

President Lincoln rejects offers of loans by the House of Rothschild and other loan sharks.

"The money powers prey upon the nation in times of peace and conspirers against it in times of adversity." - Abraham Lincoln

President Abraham Lincoln in 1861 was faced with financing the Civil War with little money. He went out to secure loans, but the best he could do were loans costing 24% to 35% interest, so he rejected their expensive offers. Lincoln then got some laws passed and had $450 million of interest-free "Greenbacks" printed. Lincoln's shunning of the money institutions such as the House of Rothschild in England and other loan sharks within the banking institutions, worldwide, all but sealed his own fate.

"The government should create, issue and circulate all of its currency and credit to satisfy the spending power of the government and the buying power of consumers...The privilege of creating and issuing money is not only a supreme prerogative of government, but it is the government's greatest creative opportunity... By the adoption of these principles, the taxpayers will save immense sums of interest...Money will cease to be master, and become servant to humanity."

-President Abraham Lincoln

"The rich rule over the poor, the barrower is servant to the lender."
- Proverbs 22:7

17

President Lincoln's statement revealed his distain towards any central banking system. In having the United States print their own currency, then issuing and regulating it, Lincoln sent shockwaves throughout England and the European banking houses. Had this policy continued, England might have followed and ended the "money reign" of then powers such as the Rothschild's and others controlling England's central bank, as well as other countries having central banking systems.

London Times
(An editorial revealing bankers, industrialists and capitalists attitude of Lincoln's actions at the time)

"If this mischievous financial policy, which has it's origin in North America, shall become indurate down to a fixture, then that government will furnish it's own money without cost. It will payoff debts, and go without debt. It will have all the money necessary to carry on its commerce. It will become prosperous without precedent in the history of the world. The brains and wealth of all countries will all go to America. That country must be destroyed, or it will destroy every monarchy in the world."

On Good Friday, April 14th, 1865, a lone gunman name John Wilks Booth assassinated President Lincoln. Booth had ordered fellow conspirators, Lewis Powell, to kill Secretary of State William H. Seward and George Atzerodt to kill Vice President Andrew Johnson. Although Booth succeeded in killing Lincoln, the larger plot failed. Seward would recover from his wounds and Vice-President Johnson's would-be assassin left Washington, D.C. upon losing his nerve.

Major Henry Rathbone, Clara Harris, Mary Todd Lincoln, President Lincoln,(left). Assassin John Wilks Booth,(right).

18

From left to right, would be assassin Lewis T. Powell, Powell attacks Fredrick Seward, Francis A. Seward and her husband William H. Seward, Secretary of State.

Of the ten conspirators, Booth was shot and died while Union soldiers attempted to arrest him 12 days after he assassinated President Lincoln. John Surratt was directly involved in the failed attempt to kidnap Lincoln days before. After the assassination, Surratt fled to Canada, then to Europe and finally arrested in Egypt 18 months after Lincoln died. After two months of trial, Surratt was ultimately released after a mistrial (eight voted innocent, four voted guilty) and the statutes of limitations had run out on lesser charges the government attempted to retry him on.

The trial of the remaining eight conspirators lasted for about seven weeks, with 366 witnesses testifying. The verdict was given on July 5 and all of the defendants were found guilty. Mary Surratt, Lewis Powell, David Herold, and George Atzerodt were sentenced to death by hanging and Samuel Mudd, Samuel Arnold, and Michael O'Laughlen were sentenced to life in prison. Edmund Spangler was sentenced to imprisonment for six years. Surratt, Powell, Herold, and Atzerodt were hanged in the Old Arsenal Penitentiary on July 7, 1865, only two days after their verdicts. Mary Surratt was the first woman to be hanged by the U.S. government. O'Laughlen died in prison of yellow fever in 1867. Mudd, Arnold, and Spangler were pardoned in February 1869 by President Johnson.

While hangman Christian Rath was placing the noose over young Powell's head he remarked "I hope you die quick." He had been impressed by Powell's courage and determination in the face of death. To this Lewis replied, "You know best captain." Lewis Powell did not die quickly as hoped by Rath. After the drop he struggled for life more than 5 minutes. His body swinging wildly, twice he "Moved his legs up into the sitting position." and was the last to die. George Atzerodt died instantly of a broken neck. David Herold gave a brief shudder and wet himself. Mary Surratt, whose neck did not break upon impact, also gave a shudder for several minutes before dying.

Note: Although only President Lincoln was assassinated, the plan was to all but eliminate the existing United States Government with also the assassination of Vice-President Johnson and Secretary of State Seward. Had Booth's plan been successful, <u>conveniently</u>, those responsible for the

London Times editorial, (On page 18.), would no longer have to worry about more of Lincoln's interest free "Greenbacks" being put into circulation.

Mary Surratt, Lewis Powell, David Herold, and George Atzerodt hanging.

Joseph and son John Kennedy

As Lincoln did 100 years before him, President Kennedy challenged the powers within the Finacial Banking Community

President Kennedy's attempt to eliminate the country's National Debt while dooming the existence of the privately owned Federal Reserve must of not only sent shockwaves through the minds of the financial institutions of J.P. Morgan, Rockefellers, Bushs and Rothschilds, but must of given them flashbacks to an earlier time when Joseph Kennedy was Chairman of the United States Securities and Exchange Commission. Under President Roosevelt, Joseph forced corporations and financial institutions selling their stock on Wall Street to make public quarterly financial statements, which ended the information monopoly that only a select few had privy to, and cost them millions of dollars in future profits. Also under Kennedy, the Commission wrote regulations for banks and financial institutions that prevented them from abusing their position until the late 1990s when they were repealed.

And like President Lincoln, President John F. Kennedy paid with his life for it!

National Banks 1863-1913

National Banks would have higher standards than the State Banks concerning reserves and business practices. The "Controller of Currency" office oversaw all National Banks to make sure they were complying with its standards and grew quickly because they had uniform currency throughout the United States. Meanwhile, many State Banks were going out of business and the ones still open, continued to pass out their own currency with less value backing it than the National Bank's currency. The National Bank imposed a 10% tax on all State Bank notes to cover losses when they honored and took out of circulation State Bank notes.

Still, two problems continued even with National Banks. Cash demands on banks in agricultural areas was seasonal, causing banks to either get loans from clearinghouse banks or call in some of their loans. In small towns, word of their bank calling in loans would travel fast which would worry depositors so much, they would withdraw their money from the bank, causing a "run" on the bank for their cash. The other problem affected all National Banks, since they were backed by treasuries that fluctuated in value, as the value of the treasuries changed so did the amount of cash and loans banks were allowed to have in circulation. When the value of treasuries went down, banks would have to call in loans or get a loan from other banks, which at times caused a "run" on their cash too.

A Clearinghouse System

Many banks survived for fifty years using a clearinghouse to acquire loans for quick cash during seasonal runs for cash, or when treasury's value went down. Also there were "fail-safe" institutions as in New York Safety Fund and Boston's Suffolk Bank. They would pool their member's cash flows to cover one another during peak times of cash demand, which worked out well to assure the depositor his money is safe.

Banking Panics of 1873, 1893 & 1907

All three "Banking Panic" started out small and snowballed into a national crisis. They could have been avoided had the president at the time stepped in quickly with cash for the floundering banks, but they didn't. In the 1873 and 1907 Panic, it was caused by pure greed of capitalist bankers that over extended themselves. In 1893, it was a lack of governmental regulations and controls on the banking and silver industry that compounded the "run" on banks to convert bank notes into silver. In retrospect, many people believed all three "Panics" were engineered by foreign capitalists and their United States "agents" to force America to go back to a central banking system. Foreign banks and financial institutions that had made fortunes as part owner of the First Bank of the United States & Second Bank of the United States, longed for over 40 years for America to return to what was their, "cash cow," a central banking system. There were also elitist bankers and industrialists that learned from American history of just how much of a "cash balloon" they could have at their disposal if they too could get in on becoming a part owner of a new United States Central Banking System. Since before the 1880s, these foreign institutions attempted to persuade people in power to get the United States back into the central banking system, but only those who would directly benefit showed interest. But when opportunity came along to aggravate a small banking crisis, they were more than willing to standby and do nothing as the crisis grew to a nationwide panic.

There were people with plans, and stood by in silence as not to be blamed.

22

In September of 1873, after a major component in the banking industry, Jay Cooke & Company, over invested in the railroad industry and was unable to market several millions of Northern Pacific Railroad bonds, he was forced to declare bankruptcy. His bankruptcy and lack of funds to payoff his investors and depositors began an epidemic of bank runs on their cash and bank defaults. As for his railroad, the Northern Pacific Railroad changed hands many times to end up in the hands of, not surprisingly, J.P. Morgan, Edward H. Harriman, and Jacob Schiff from the firm of Kuhn, Loeb & Company of Germany.

One of the contributing factors to the 1907 Panic was F. Augustine Heinze and his attempted entrance into the "banker's elite" of New York. After selling his copper mine in Montana, he moved to New York and bought Knickerbocker Trust and became director of the financial chain. Meanwhile banking industry leaders, threatened by Heinze's developing trusts, staged a financial attack on Knickerboxer Trust to sway public opinion against trusts. Heinze at the same time and out of desperation to save his Trust Company, with large loans from Knickerbocker Trust, unsuccessfully attempted to corner United Copper during a time when money was already extremely tight. Shortly thereafter, National Bank of Commerce, controlled by the Rockefeller Family, refused to honor Kickerbocker Trust checks, causing a run on their bank, then snowballed to other trust institutions, just as the banking elites of New York had planned. Earlier in the year, a planned Stock Market crash occurred that scarcely affected those elitists in the know, but to the common investor and those that weren't privy to reports and inside information that the elitists had, it cost them greatly. To the elite capitalists and foreign investors, "runs on the bank's cash" that caused banks to call in loans normally didn't effect their empires. They would, as they do today, look at the country's depression as only an opportunity to buy land and businesses for pennies on the dollar while their financial institutions took the loss to avoid paying taxes.

> *"I always tried to turn every disaster into an opportunity."*
> **- John D. Rockefeller (1839-1937)**

These elitists of capitalism live in a world unbeknown to the common individual. Money count is secondary to their achievement against fellow upper-class members.

> *"Money was never a big motivation for me, except for a way to keep score. The real excitement is playing the game."*
> **- Donald Trump**

Benjamin Harrison, President 1889-1893

Signed the Sherman Antitrust Act that put a limit on individuals, corporations and businesses to have cartels and monopolies, which they were useing to monipulate their markets for higher prices and profits.

During President Reagan's Administration beginning in January of 1981, and continued through Presidents George Bush Sr., Bill Clinton and G.W. Bush Jr.'s Administrations, the Sherman Antitrust Act was all but ignored. Corporations were allowed to buy their competition with their taxable profits to avoid paying taxes while forming monopolies and cartels to manipulate markets with higher prices for increased profit. Nowhere was this more prevalent than when two of John D. Rockefeller's original oil companies which the Rockefeller Family still owned a substantial amount of stock in, Exxon and Mobil oil companies, surprisingly were allowed to merge in 1999 into ExxonMobil Oil Company. (John D. Rockefeller was forced, under the Sherman Antitrust Act, to break up his Standard Oil Company that at the time was considered a monopoly by the United States Supreme Court in 1911 because it had grown to supply at one time as much as 91% of gasoline & oil to the United States. Rockefeller retained at least 25% of the 32 companies that was created when breaking up Standard Oil. Two of these 32 companies, Jersey Standard & Socony, also known a Standard Oil Company of New York, would later be called Exxon and Mobil, respectively.)

President William McKinley
25th President of the United States
In office: March 4th, 1897 to September 14th, 1901

William McKinley's campaign for president was well financed by industrialist Marcus Hanna. Hanna years earlier had befriended a young John D. Rockefeller in 1844 when they attended Cleveland Central High School together and became life long friends and business associates.

With the help of big business, McKinley won the presidential election in 1896 on a platform of a gold standard for currency and high tariffs. In his first term, he signed the "Dingley Act" in 1897 that raised tariffs to an average of 46% and as high as 57% on some imports. The high tariffs protected McKinley's big business financial backers from foreign competition while they increased their prices for high profits. The bigger they got, the more of the market share they wanted. When they came up against domestic competition in a particular market, they would lower their prices in that market only, and until, they drive their competition out of business. After all their competition either went bankrupt or sold to them for pennies-on-the-dollar, they raise their prices for high profits.

McKinley won re-election over William Jennings Bryan, who accused him for allowing big business to control their markets with illegal monopolies.

At the beginning of his second term, McKinley had a change of heart toward high tariffs. After seeing how big business was taking an unfair advantage of independent businesses both foreign and domestic, he no longer supported protective tariffs and was open to free commerce and fairer trade agreements.

President McKinley with wife arrives at the Pan American Exposition.

President McKinley with wife arrived at the Pan American Exposition in Buffalo, New York on September 5th, 1901. The Exposition was celebrating 100 years of progress in North and South America. McKinley delivered a speech on his new positions on tariffs and trade, which was to lower tariff rates and be more open to new trade agreements. This was much to the dislike of his past financial, big-business backers that was responsible for him being in office and benefited financially from high tariff rates. On the second day at the Exposition, September 6th, President McKinley stood in the Temple of Music greeting people from a line that had formed to shake his hand. Leon Frank Czolgosz approached McKinley and fired two shots which eventually killed him.

"Lights Out in the City of Light"
Anarchy and Assassination
at the Pan-American Exposition

Hundreds gathered at the Exposition Hospital for the latest news.

On September 14th, 1901, McKinley would be pronounced dead at 2:15 A.M., his assassin, Leon Frank Czolgosz as the government then news media called him instead of just Frank Czolgosz, was convicted during an eight and a half hour "kangaroo-court style trial" on September 23rd and executed only five weeks later.

Czolgosz an assassin or patsy?

Forewarning by the Anarchist group of Leon Frank Czolgosz!

"*The attention of the comrades is called to another spy. Frank Czolgosz is well dressed, medium height, rather narrow shouldered and about 25 years old. Up to the present he has made himself known in Chicago and Cleveland. In the former place, he stayed a short time, while in Cleveland he disappeared when our comrades confirmed themselves of his identity and were at the point interested in our caus, asking for names...If this individual makes his appearance elsewhere, the comrades are warned in advance, and can act accordingly.*"

Assassin Leon Frank Czolgosz was painted as an anarchist by the government, but there was no proof the group accepted him as a member; only a person the group should look at as a spy and to avoid. On September 23rd, 1901, he was convicted during an eight and a half hour trial from jury selection to sentencing. He was executed October 29th, 1901.

Decades later, another accused assassin's background would not match up with what the government wanted the public to beleive; a communist, an anti-communist... pro-Castro, anti-Castro... Disinformation on Oswald to confuse the public, a CIA-Allen Dulles plan.

Lee Oswald

"I'm a patsy!" declared Oswald.

Chapter III
The Federal Reserve privately owned Central System

Federal Reserve Central Banking System

**Nelson Aldrich (left) John D. Rockefeller Jr., (middle) and
Aldrich's daughter, Abby, who married John D. Rockefeller Jr.**

Nelson Aldrich was considered the most powerful politician of his time. A leader of the Republican Party in the Senate, Nelson was the central member of the Senate Finance Committee. Known by the public and press as the "Nation's General Manager," he influenced all policies on tariffs and monetary. Aldrich rebuilt the American Financial

System, sponsored and pushed through the Federal Income Tax Amendment and the Federal Reserve Act. Always known as a close friend to the capitalists, he sold his vast railroad interest to J.P. Morgan. His daughter, Abby, married John D. Rockefeller Jr., and the two would be parents to the famous five Rockefeller sons.

The Federal Reserve would be a third try at a central banking system for America, following the "First & Second Bank of the United States," which all but bankrupted the country. For reasons of past corruption, careless speculation and favoritism by the first two central bank owners toward corporations over small businesses, the farmers and individual depositors, most people were against going back to a central banking system. For decades, European banking institutions such as the Rothschilds, Warburgs and Kuhn Loeb & Company tried to convince American politicians with bribery to pass a privately owned central banking system, but their opponents always prevailed. Powerful capitalists as Rockefellers, Harrimans, Bushs and J.P. Morgan also attempted to convince the country a central banking system was needed, while in private among themselves, they were eyeing huge profits from large loans for their own financial and industrial empires if such a banking system ever became law under their ownership.

In 1908, Senate Republican Party leader Nelson Aldrich was the chief sponsor of the Aldrich-Vreeland Act which created the National Monetary Commission. The record shows that Senator Aldrich divided the Commission into two groups; one would study the United States Banking System while Aldrich's group would travel throughout Europe and South America to study their banking systems. Some would later say Aldrich's group travels was more like a vacation paid for by the government and that their plan for a Central Banking System was cast in stone by foreign bankers. Most of the 250 reports submitted by the Commission's groups between 1908 and 1911 were ignored in favor of plans Aldrich and his elitist friends had for the new United States central banking system.

Jekyll Island Club

In 1885, Newton Finney had plans to make Jekyll Island from a once agricultural plantation into a winter resort for the powerful and wealthy. Finney's brother-in-law, John Eugene Dubignon, had ownership of one-third of the island. After the two got financing and became owners of the entire island, they with other influential men, petitioned Glynn county courts to incorporate the Island. Then Finney signed an agreement to sell the Island to the Jekyll Island Club. Shares of the Club were sold to only the rich and powerful including, J.P. Morgan Jr., Henry Hyde, Marshall Field, Joseph Pulitzer and William H. Vanderbilt.

Secret meeting at the Jekyll Island Club

Their mission was to form a privately owned, central banking system, by which those they represented would have control in monopoly form of the United State currency.

Those attending, their titles and who they represented.

Nelson Aldrich	Edward M. House	Henry P. Davison	Charles D. Norton
Senator	*Pres. Wilson Advisor*	*Senior Partner*	*Pres. J.P. Morgan*
John D. Rockefeller		J.P. Morgan	

Benjamin Strong	Frank A. Vanderlip	Paul M. Warburg	Abraham Andrew
V.P. J.P. Morgan	*Pres. of Rockefeller Bank*	*Partner of Kuhn, Loeb & Co.*	*Asst. Sec. of Treasury*

Paul Warburg also represented his brother's *Warburg Banking of Germany, House of Rothschild* and *Bank of England.*

What they created would change the world forever...

What they would later say about their meeting at Jekyll Island Club.

Frank A. Vanderlip, President of Rockefeller's National City Bank of New York wrote in *"The Saturday Evening Post,"* Feb. 6, issues the following.

"Despite my views about the values to society of greater publicity for the affairs of corporations, there was an occasion, near the close of 1910, when I was as secretive – indeed, a furtive – as any conspirator...I do not feel it is any exaggeration to speak of our secret expedition to Jekyll Island as the occasion of the actual conception of what eventually became the Federal Reserve System. We were told to leave our last names behind us. We were told, further, that we should avoid dining together on the night of our departure. We were instructed to come one at a time and as unobtrusively as possible to the railroad terminal on the New Jersey littoral of the Hudson, where Senator Aldrich's private car would be in readiness, attached to the rear end of the train for the South...Once aboard the private car, we began to observe the taboo that had been fixed on last names. We addressed one another as "Ben," "Paul," "Nelson," "Abe" – it is Abraham Piatt Andrew. Davison and I adopted even deeper disguises, abandoning our first names. On the theory that we were always right, he became Wilbur and I became Orville, after those two aviation pioneers, the Wright Brothers. The servants and train crew may have known the identities of one or two of us, but they did not know all, and it was the names of all printed together that would of made our mysterious journey significant in Washington, in Wall Street, even in London. Discovery, we knew, simply must not happen, or else our time and effort would be wasted. If it were to be exposed publicly that our particular group had gotten together and written a banking bill, that bill would have no chance whatever of passage by Congress. As with all cartels, it had to be created by legislation and sustained by the power of government under the deception of protecting the consumers."

Paul Warburg was credited with writing the bill, a partner of Kuhn, Loeb & Company, and also represented the House of Rothschild from England, Germany & France, Bank of England, and his brother, Max Warburg, Warburg Banking consortium from Germany & Netherlands. Warburg in 1930 wrote in his book, *The Federal Reserve System, Its Origin and Growth*; which the follow quote came from.

31

"The results of the conference were entirely confidential. Even the fact there had been a meeting was not permitted to become public...Though eighteen years have since gone by, I do not feel free to give a description of this most interesting conference concerning which Senator Aldrich pledged all participants to secrecy."

Debate over a new Central Banking System Bill

First Proposal: Aldrich Plan would have fifteen regional banks, nationwide, to be coordinated by a board of commercial bankers. This so called National Reserve Association Regional Banks would make emergency loans to smaller, local bank members throughout their region to avoid cash flow seasonal shortages that would end any "banking panics" of the past with "runs" of local bank's cash flow. The National Reserve Association would also create money and act as fiscal agents for the United States Government.

Objection to the Aldrich Plan: Since the *Aldrich Plan* essentially gave full control of the United States Currency System to a small group of private bankers, there was widespread opposition to the Plan in fear it would become a tool for the elitist rich and the more influential financiers.

Second Proposal: Glass-Owen Bill would service the smaller local banks much in the same way as the *Aldrich Plan.* But the *Glass-Owen Bill* would establish a Federal Reserve Board that has controlling interest, create a new Federal Reserve Notes by the United States Treasury, and National Banks would be required to join.

Objection to the Glass-Owen Bill: Opposition to the *Glass-Owen Bill* came mostly from Republicans, many of which were "agents" for the powerful elitist's financiers of New York, which also had their "agents" representing them on Jekyll Island when the *Aldrich Plan* was written.

Alfred Crozier, lawyer, author of 1912 book "U.S. Money vs Corporation Currency."

Testified for the Senate Committee, attacking the Aldrich-Vreeland Plan Act of 1908 as a tool of Wall Street and with a private own central bank system, the nation would no longer be free.

"It should prohibit the calling in of loans for the purpose of influencing quotation prices of securities and the contracting of loans or increasing interest rates in concert by the banks to influence public opinion or any legislative body. Within recent months, William McAdoo, Secretary of the

Treasury of the United States was reported in the open press as charging specifically that there was a conspiracy among certain of the large banking interests to put a contraction upon the currency and to raise interest rates for the sake of making the public to force Congress into passing currency legislation desired by those interests".

"The so-called administration currency bill grants just what Wall Street and the big banks for twenty-five years have been striving for, that are, PRIVATE INSTEAD OF PUBLIC CONTROL OF CURRENCY. It does this as completely as the Aldrich Bill. Both measures rob the government and the people of all effective control of the public's money, and vest in the banks exclusively the dangerous power to make money among the people scarce or plenty. The Aldrich Plan put this power in one central bank. The Administration Plan put it into twelve regional banks, all owned exclusively by the identical private interests that would have owned and operated the Aldrich Bank."

Pujo Committee Hearings

From May of 1912 to January of 1913, the Pujo Committee, a sub-committee of the House Committee on Banking and Currency held investigative hearings. Renowned corporate lawyer Samuel Untermyer was hired to conduct what would be later described as **"hearings to sell a form of centralized banking system to the public."** Untermyer, who would later take an active role in writing the "Federal Reserve Act," totally controlled the hearings calling on elitist financiers such as J.P. Morgan to testify on their own behalf. But the end result to the Hearings, from Untermyer's manipulation of the witnesses and newspapers, was that observers to the Hearings came away more confused than with sound truths.

"The Aldrich Plan is a Wall Street Plan. It means another panic, if necessary, to intimidate the people. Aldrich, paid by the government to represent the people, proposes a plan for the trusts instead. A radical is one that speaks the truth. This Act establishes the most gigantic trust on Earth. When the President signs this Bill, the invisible government by the Monetary Power will be legalized... The people may not know it immediately but the day of reckoning is only a few years removed...The worst legislative crime of the ages is perpetrated by this banking bill."
- Congressman Charles Lindbergh Sr.

For months in 1913, there were congressional hearings and debates that gave the public as much disinformation as sound truth to what was really being proposed. It became more of a war of words between the **powerful elitist's bankers and their agents** vs. **those against handing over the United States Currency System to the same elitist's bankers.** Congressional Committees took votes and added amendments, with little really being accomplished to sway either side.

"The great banks for years have sought and have control agents in the Treasury to serve their purposes. Let me quote from the <u>World</u> Article. Just as soon as Mr. McAdoo came to Washington, a woman whom the National City Bank had installed in the Treasury Department to get advance information on the condition of the banks, and other matters of interest to the big Wall Street group, was removed. Immediately the Secretary and Assistant Secretary were criticized severely by the agents of the Wall Street group. I myself have known on more than one occasion when banks have refused credit to men opposed to their political views and purposes. When Senator Aldrich and others were going around the country exploiting this scheme, the big banks of New York and Chicago were engaged in raising a munificent fund to bolster up the Aldrich propaganda. I have been told by bankers of my own state that contributions to this exploitation fund had been demanded of them and that they had contributed because they were afraid of being blacklisted or boycotted. There are bankers of this country who are enemies of the public's welfare. In the past, a few great banks have followed the policies and projects that have paralyzed industrial energies of the country to perpetrate their tremendous power over the financial and business industries of America." - Senator Stone

"I'm also suggesting the Central Board lengthen their term from eight to ten years. This would take away the power of the President to change the personnel of the Board during one term in office." - Edward House to Col. Garrison, agent for Brown Brothers; later to be Brown Brothers, Harriman.

By mid-December of 1913, there was a Federal Reserve Act proposed for legislation. Word got out to only those known to be against the proposal as written, that action on it would be set aside until after the Christmas break. Then on December 22, 1913, when the congressmen that were fed disinformation that a vote on the Federal Reserve Act was put off until after the first of the year had went home for Christmas break and wouldn't take part in the vote, the House passed the Federal Reserve Act easily with 298 yeas to 60 nays and 76 not voting. Members of the Senate for months was a stumbling block over any kind of centralized banking system and was insistent of waiting until after Christmas break to take a vote. But the influential Senator Aldrich and his cronies were very persistent in attaining a quorum and vote before they left town. On the eve of Christmas Eve, Aldrich forced a vote to be taken in the Senate, which passed 43 to 25 with 27 not there to vote. The record shows that all that didn't get an opportunity to vote, because they deviously were misled to believe the vote would take place after their Christmas break, had previously declared their intentions of opposing the Federal Reserve Act Bill. Had the 27 absent Senators voted, the Federal Reserve Act would have failed to pass. Later that day, President Wilson signed into law the Federal Reserve Act which would be made public on Christmas Eve.

"If the American people ever allow private banks to control the issuance of their currency, first by inflation, then by deflation, the banks and corporations that will grow up around them, will deprive the people of all their property until their children will wake up homeless on the continent their fathers conquered." - Thomas Jefferson

Federal Reserve Central Banking System Becomes Law!

DECEMBER 24, 1913—SIXTEEN PAGES. — PRICE TWO CENTS

PRESIDENT'S SIGNATURE -ENACTS CURRENCY LAW

Wilson Declares It the First of Series of Constructive Acts to Aid Business.

Makes Speech to Group of Democratic Leaders.

Conference Report Adopted in Senate by Vote of 43 to 25.

Banks All Over the Country Hasten to Enter Federal Reserve System.

Gov-Elect Walsh Calls Passage of Bill A Fine Christmas Present.

WILSON SEES DAWN OF NEW ERA IN BUSINESS

Aims to Make Prosperity Free to Have Unimpeded Momentum.

HOME VIEWS OF CURRENCY ACT   FOUR PENS USED BY PRESIDENT

Christmas came early to the banker elitists!

The **_Aldrich-Vreeland Act of 1908_** was passed to establish the *National Monetary Commission* to solve "banking panics" and bank shortages of cash that cause "runs" on their cash flows. For the next five-and-a-half years, there were endless investigations, over 250 reports, hearings, debates, propaganda and misinformation over a new *Central Banking System* for the United States. Late December of 1913, Senator Aldrich, a past business associate of J.P. Morgan and father in-law to John D. Rockefeller Jr., felt voting and passing the proposed **_Federal Reserve Act_** before 1914 was so important that he used all of his political capital and called in all favors owed to him by friends to rush the most important legislation in the history of the country to a vote, which before the vote, he knew he would win. Some politicians and newspapers would later accuse Aldrich of not only being an "agent" for the Rockefeller Family and J.P. Morgan, but said he insisted on the Senate vote because he had manipulated 27 Senators out of town for the Christmas break to assure the pro-business, pro-elitist's banker **_Federal Reserve Act Bill_** would pass.

The Federal Reserve Act of 1913

The Federal Reserve Act created a central banking system with 12 regional branches and a new currency called the Federal Reserve Note, with entities both private and public ownership of stock. The Federal Reserve will have a Federal Reserve Board of seven members appointed by the President, (which was changed and renamed in 1935 to a Board of Governors of the Federal Reserve System, and to drop from the Board the United States Secretary of the Treasury and Comptroller of the Currency). Each regional bank will have a board of directors and regional boundaries. All nationally chartered banks would be required to become members of the Federal Reserve System, purchase specific amount of non-transferable stock in the regional Federal Reserve Bank, and deposit a stipulated amount of non-interest bearing reserves with their Federal Reserve Regional Bank. State chartered banks would be allowed to join at their wish with the same requirements as the National Banks, and be in-part under the supervision of the Federal Reserve. Member banks would be entitled to discount loans from the Federal Reserve Regional Banks. The Federal Reserve Act also makes the Federal Reserve fiscal agents of the United States Government.

"This is the strangest, most dangerous advantage ever placed in the hands of privilege class by any Government that ever existed. The system is private, conducted for the sole purpose of obtaining the greatest possible profits from the use of other people's money. They know in advance when to create panics to their advantage. They also know when to stop panics. Inflation and deflation work equally well for them when they control finance." - Congressman Charles A. Lindbergh Sr.

"Before the passage of this Act, the New York bankers could only dominate the reserves of New York. Now we are able to dominate the bank reserves of the entire country."

- Senator Nelson W. Aldrich,
    Father in-law to John D. Rockefeller Jr.

"In the Federal Reserve Law, they have wrested from the people and secured for themselves the constitutional power to issue money and regulate the value thereof. The House of Morgan is now in supreme control of our industry, commerce and political affairs. They are in complete control of the policy making of the Democratic, Republican and Progressive parties. The present extraordinary propaganda for 'preparedness' is planned more for home coercion than for defense against foreign aggression." — Henry L. Loucks, Author, Politician

The rich rule over the poor,
the barrower is servant to the lender."
        - Proverbs 22:7

"In practice, the Federal Reserve Bank of New York became the fountainhead of the system of twelve regional banks, for New York was the money market of the nation. The other eleven banks were just expensive mausoleums erected to salve the local pride and quell the Jacksonian fears of the hinterland. Benjamin Strong, president of J.P. Morgan's Banker Trust, was selected as the first Governor of the New York Federal Reserve Bank. Adept in high finance, Strong for many years manipulated the country's monetary system at the discretion of directors representing the leading New York Banks. Under Strong, the Reserve System was brought into interlocking relations with the Bank of England and the Bank of France. Benjamin Strong held his position as Governor of the Federal Reserve Bank of New York until his sudden death in 1928, during a Congressional investigation of the secret meetings between Reserve Governors and heads of European central banks which brought on the Great Depression of 1929-31."
        - Ferdinand Lundberg, from "The Sixty's Families"

"The purpose of the Federal Reserve Act was to prevent the concentration of money in the New York Banks by making it profitable for country bankers to use their funds at home, but the movement of currency shows that the New York banks gained from the interior in every month except December, 1915, since the Act went into effect. The stabilization of rates has taken place in New York alone. In other parts, high rates continue. The Act, which was to deprive Wall Street of its funds for speculation, has really given the bulls and bears such a supply as they never had before."

"The truth is that far from having clogged the channel to Wall Street, as Mr. Glass so confidently boasted, it actually widened the old channels and opened up two new ones. The first of these leads directly to Washington and gives Wall Street a string on all the surplus cash in the United States Treasury. Besides, in the power to issue bank-note currency, it furnishes an inexhaustible supply of credit money; the second channel leads to the great central banks of Europe, whereby, through the sale of acceptances, virtually guaranteed by the United States Government, Wall Street in granted immunity from foreign demands of gold which have precipitated every great crisis in our history."

- W.H. Allen wrote in *Moody's Magazine*, 1916

To his dieing day, President Woodrow Wilson regretted signing the Federal Reserve Act. He said after leaving office, that he was misinformed prior to signing the bill by people he had trusted. That he would of never signed it had he know then, what he knows now.

Chapter IV
Major Stockholders of the Federal Reserve

House of Rothschild (Banks in England & Germany) Rothschild Family

1805-Present, Banks throughout Europe, International Finance, their agents:
J.P. Morgan, Rockefellers, Harriman. Funded governments for wars
Today: Concordia BV (Holding co. when Paris & London banks merged.)
Rothschild et Cie Banque controls banking businesses in Europe.
Rothschild Continuation Holdings AG controls banking worldwide.
N.M. Rothschild, (under above), does mostly mergers & acquisitions.
LCF Rothschild Group, Geneva, Switzerland, extends 15 countries.
(The Group's primary businesses include the 3 listed below, that are mostly
financial entities dealing with asset management and private banking. They
also cover winemaking, luxury hotels, mixed farming and yacht racing).
Banque Privee Edmond de Rothschild S.A.
La Campagnie Benjamin de Rothschild S.A.
COGIFRANCE
Rothschild Investment Trust
(RIT Capital Partners, the UK's Largest investment trust.)
J. Rothschild Assurance Group, (now St. James's Place Capital).

Warburg Banks (Germany & Netherlands) Max Warburg Family

1798-Present, Hamburg, Germany. Private investment bank.
Today: M.M. Warburg CO, large private investment bank.
IG Farben industrial conglomerate but lost it to Nazis by 1938.
(Max Warburg's brother, Paul Warburg known as creator & "Father" to the
United States Federal Reserve System. Felix Warburg, New York banker).
Warburg Pincus, (E.M. Warburg & Co. blocked), 1938, New York, a private
equity firm. 1970 named E.M. Warburg, Pincus & Co.
S.G. Warburg & Co., 1946, major UK investment bank

Kuhn, Loeb Company (Germany) Abraham Kuhn and Solomon Loeb

1867-1977, Investment bank & service, management & banking 2nd only to J.P.
Morgan Company,
financially banked E.H. Harriman
1920s & 30s German, later Nazi connection with Harriman & Bush Families.
1977 Merged with Lehman Brothers.
1984 After Lehman Brothers & American Express merged, name dropped.
Today: Out of business.

J.P. Morgan Company

1861 Founded by J. Pierpont Morgan, served as an agent office in New York to write European securities for the firm his father works at, George Peabody Company of London, England.

1864 Junius Spencer Morgan takes over George Peabody Co. after owner dies and names it J.S. Morgan Company.

1871 J.P. Morgan and Anthony Drexel form merchant banking partnership named Drexel Morgan & Company.

1885 J.P. Morgan invests in railroads and telephone companies.

1895 J.P. Morgan saves United States Government from default with gold.

1895 Drexel dies, J.S. Morgan, Drexel Morgan & Co., and Morgan Harjes Co. reorganized to form J.P. Morgan & Company.

1901 J.P. Morgan makes industrialist Andrew Carnegie richest man in world by buying him out and combining 33 companies to form United States Steel, the 1st billion dollar corporation.

1907 J.P. Morgan saves New York City from default by buying $30 million of N.Y. City's bonds while saving brokerage house with financing; although some believe this was caused by elitist bankers to get people thinking of returning to a central banking system. If true, it worked.

1913 J.P. Morgan Company buys stock in Federal Reserve Bank.

1913 J.P. Morgan dies, J.P. Morgan Jr. takes over.

1915 J.P. Morgan Co. acts as U.S. agent for British & French Government to

acquire arms for war that Samuel Bush directs, George Sr.'s grandpa.

1940 Company goes public.

1959 Merge with Guaranty Trust Co. to form Morgan Guaranty Trust Co.

1968 Founded Morgan Euroclear of Brussels, a system for settlements and services to Eurobond securities.

1989 Federal Reserve allows J.P. Morgan Co. to deal with corporate debt.

1990 Restructures Mexico's $50 billion debt.

2000 Formed Euroclear Bank in Brussels, largest international clearing system in world.

2000 Merge with Chase Manhattan Bank naming it JP Morgan Chase Co.

2004 Merge with Bank One.

2005 Form JP Morgan Cazenove Limited, an investment banking partnership.

2008 Bought Bear Stearns.

Today: Leading global financial services firm in 50 countries and assets of over $1.5 trillion.

Lazard Brothers Banks, (New York), Alexander, Simon & Elie Lazard.

1848 Founded in New Orleans, LA. In dry goods, moved to San Francisco as an import-export co.

1858 Expanded into banking & foreign exchange businesses and opened Paris, France office.

1870 opened London, England office.

1876 provided solely financial services.

Today: May of 2005 went public, ending over 150 years of private ownership. Parent company of Lazard LLC, based in New York with offices in Europe, North America, Asia and Austria with over 2,200 employees. Investment banking are participates in mergers & acquisitions. Lazard Capital Markets, 2005, investment bank.

Chase Manhattan Bank (New York) John D. Rockefeller

1799 The Manhattan Company founded by Aaron Burr.

1877 Chase National Bank founded by John Thompson in 1877. John D. Rockefeller Jr. and Family would become their largest stockholder.

1955 Chase & Manhattan Banks merged.

1969 Became part of a holding company under David Rockefeller named Chase Manhattan Corp.

1996 Purchased by Chemical Bank.

2000 Purchased J.P. Morgan & Co. renamed JPMorgan Chase & Co.

Today: JP Morgan Chase & Co., largest credit card co. in U.S. and 3rd Largest bank in assets.

Lehman Brothers (New York) Emanuel & Mayer Lehman

1850 Founded, trading their dry goods for cotton.

1858 Expanded and Emanuel relocated to New York.

1862 Teamed up with John Durr and renamed to Lehman, Durr & Co.

1870 Headquarters to New York & founded New York Cotton Exchange and dealt in railroad bonds and financial advisory business.

1883 Member of Coffee Exchange.

1887 Member of New York Stock Exchange.

1890 Developed international interests in Europe & Japan.

1977 Merged with Kuhn, Loeb & Co to form Lehman Brothers, Kuhn, Loeb & Inc.

Today: Lehman Brothers Holding Inc. as of 1994, equities, investments.

George Herbert Walker IV of Bush Family is Director.

Goldman Sachs, (New York) Marcus Goldman & Samuel Sachs

1869-Present founded by Marcus Goldman for commercial paper (money)
1896 Joined New York Stock Exchange.
1896 Goldman added son in-law, Samuel Sachs to firm.
1929 Goldman Sachs Trading Corporation started dealing with closed-end mutual

funds, but fail with the New York Stock crash the same year.
1970s Went international with 1st office in London.
1980s Acquired J. Aron & Company, added commodities trading.
1986 Goldman Sachs Asset Management manages mutual & hedge funds.
2004-2006 Sold short against housing market, averted mortgage debacle.
Today: One of the largest investment banks in the world.

National City Bank, New York, (Rockefeller)

1812 Founded as City Bank of New York by a group of merchants headed by
Samuel Osgood, who had been U.S. Postmaster General.
1865 Named National Bank of New York after joining national banking system
1894 Considered one of largest banks in United States.
1897 1st major bank to add foreign department.
1905 J.P. Morgan, under House of Rothschild, becomes major stockholders.
1913 1st stockholder of Federal Reserve.
1955 Renamed to First National Bank of New York.
1976 Renamed Citibank
Today: Major international investment bank with assets in 2005 of $1.5 trillion.

*Samuel Bush was on the Board of Directors and major stockholder of the Federal Reserve Regional Bank of Cleveland, Ohio…and the Bush Family retained stock after his death.

The Federal Reserve Act must surely rank as one of the most disastrous and outrageous pieces of legislation to the public welfare ever to come out of any legislative body. It was also illegal according to Article 1, Section 8 of the Constitution. The article states that *Congress shall have the power to coin (create) money and regulate the value thereof. In 1935, the US Supreme Court ruled that Congress cannot constitutionally delegate its power to another group or body.* Congress thus acted in violation of the Constitution it's sworn to uphold and in so doing created the Federal Reserve System that is a private for-profit corporation operating at the expense of the public welfare. By its action, our lawmakers committed fraud against the people of the country and so far have gotten away with it without the public even knowing about the harm done.

President John F. Kennedy would also believe the Federal Reserve System as unconstitutional for Congress to hand over the responsibility of creating, printing, issuing and regulating the United States Currency to private banking institutions.

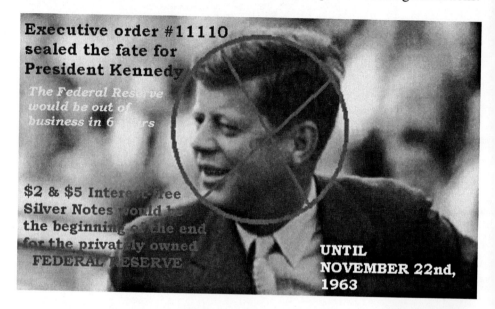

Executive order #11110 sealed the fate for President Kennedy

The Federal Reserve would be out of business in 6 ... rs

$2 & $5 Interest free Silver Notes would be the beginning of the end for the privately owned FEDERAL RESERVE

UNTIL NOVEMBER 22nd, 1963

"We shall have world government, whether or not we like it. The only question is whether world government will be achieved by conquest or consent." Paul Warburg author of Federal Reserve Act

"The Federal Reserve is a fount of credit, not of capital."
- Paul Warburg

"The way to control governments, businesses and population is not to become richer than they, as much as, leering them into becoming indebted to you. The possession of unlimited power will make a despot of almost any man. There is a possible Nero in the gentlest of human creature that walks." - **Nelson Aldrich**

The elitist powers of the time were also owners and investors of international empires in industry, banking institutions and influential stockholders of the United States Federal Reserve. They controlled the largest pool of money in the world, which was what they had worked and schemed for since their agents met on Jekyll Island in 1910. Now they could use their influence in the Federal Reserve to gain loans for their own industrial and banking empires, and to loan and indebt those governments, businesses and populations around the world. Once the elitists would get others to fall prey to the temptations of their money loaning deals that would get them into debt, they would be under the control of, and become "pawns" to, the elitist stockholders of the United States Federal Reserve, a trap as old as Adam & Eve's apple.

President John F. Kennedy would pay with his life for challenging the powers behind the United States Federal Reserve with Executive Order 11110.
No president since has had the courage, as JFK did, to put the United States Constitution above the capitalist bankers and their control of the Federal Reserve.

The Federal Reserve was divided into 12 regions, with all National Banks required to join. To give the delusion that the powerful bankers of New York wouldn't be running the Federal Reserve as they had with the "First & Second United States Central Banks," they had Board of Governors for the entire System. They also had Regional Board of Directors that gave the illusion they too would have some say the way the Federal Reserve handled the U. S. Government's money collected from taxes and tariffs.

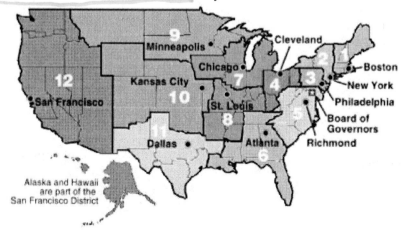

Chapter V
Yet Another Would Challenge the Powerful Money Changers

Thomas Jefferson   James Madison   Andrew Jackson   Abraham Lincoln

Up until June 10th of 1932, only two United States Presidents had directly interfered with the country's central banking system. Thomas Jefferson despised the central banking system as an "un-Godly tool for speculation, manipulation and corruption." After being elected as President in 1801, by 1804 Jefferson had withdrawn all of the government's money from the central bank, thus crippling its existence. The First Bank of the United States' charter expired in 1811 and the central bank finally closing in 1815.

"I sincerely believe that banking institutions are more dangerous to our liberties than standing armies. Already they have raised up a money aristocracy that has set the government at defiance. The issuing power should be taken from the banks and restored to the people to whom it properly belongs.

–Thomas Jefferson

"I place the economy among the first and most important virtues and debt as the greatest of dangers to be feared."
                                                        Thomas Jefferson

After Andrew Jackson became President of the United States in 1828, he too pulled out the government's money from the Central Bank in 1836 and all but dooming the Second Bank of the United States future. Twice, there would be assassination attempts on President Jackson to stop him.

"...beyond question, this great and powerful institution have been actively engaged in attempting to influence the election of public officers with its money."

- President Andrew Jackson

As an example of how the elitist bankers had dictated the country's policy, hard economic times, and in-part caused by the banker's reluctance to loan the United States Government money, forced a very reluctant President James Madison, 1809-1817, into signing a centralized banking bill out of desperation to raise currency during the 1812 War.

"History records that the Money Changers have used every form of abuse, intrigue, deceit and violent means possible to maintain their control over governments by controlling money and their issuance." - James Madison

President Abraham Lincoln, 1861–1865, on the other hand didn't have to deal with the scheming greed of a central bank. But he was in need of money to pay for a Civil War that divided the country like it had never been divided it before. Lincoln had signed the Revenue Act of 1861 that was a Federal income tax of 3% from income over $800, and 5% from all living outside of the country, but it wasn't enough to fund the Civil War. The Revenue Act of 1862 increased income tax to only those making over $10,000 to 5%, but wasn't enough. Lincoln rejected loan offers domestic and foreign that carried the outrageous interest rates of 24% to 35%.

"The money powers prey upon the nation in times of peace, and conspires against it in times of adversity." - Abraham Lincoln

Lincoln's answer to the rising cost of the Civil War was for the United States Government to print and issue their money. In 1862, Lincoln ordered $430 million in "Lincoln's Greenbacks."

"The government should create, issue and circulate all of its currency and credit to satisfy the spending power of the government and the buying power of consumers...The privilege of creating and issuing money is not only a supreme prerogative of government, but it is the government's greatest creative opportunity... By the adoption of these principles, the taxpayers will save immense sums of interest...Money will cease to be master, and become servant to humanity." - President Lincoln

The only Congressman to ever challenge the Federal Reserve

Louis Thomas McFadden
July 25th, 1876 - October 1st, 1936
1914-33 Elected to 10 two year terms to the
United States House of Representatives.
1920-31 Chairman of the United States
House Committee on Banking & Currency.

In 1933, Congressman, Louis T. McFadden, brought formal charges against the Board of Governors of the Federal Reserve Bank system, the Comptroller of the Currency and the Secretary of United States Treasury for numerous criminal acts, including but not limited to, CONSPIRACY, FRAUD, UNLAWFUL CONVERSION AND TREASON.

The following is MacFadden's speech to Congress.

"Mr. Chairman, we have in this Country one of the most corrupt institutions the world has ever known. I refer to the Federal Reserve Board and the Federal Reserve Banks, hereinafter called the Fed. The Fed has cheated the Government of these United States and the people of the United States out of enough money to pay the Nation's debt. The depredations and iniquities of the Fed have cost enough money to pay the National debt several times over. This evil institution has impoverished and ruined the people of these United States, has bankrupted itself, and has practically bankrupted our Government. It has done this through the defects of the law under which it operates, through the maladministration of that law by the Fed and through the corrupt practices of the moneyed vultures who control it."

"Some people who think that the Federal Reserve Banks are United States Government institutions. They are private monopolies which prey upon the people of these United States for the benefit of themselves and their foreign customers; foreign and domestic speculators and swindlers; and rich and predatory money lender. In that dark crew of financial pirates there are those who would cut a man's throat to get a dollar out of his pocket; there are those

who send money into states to buy votes to control our legislatures; there are those who maintain International propaganda for the purpose of deceiving us into granting of new concessions which will permit them to cover up their past misdeeds and set again in motion their gigantic train of crime."

"These twelve private credit monopolies were deceitfully and disloyally foisted upon this Country by the bankers who came here from Europe and repaid us our hospitality by undermining our American institutions. Those bankers took money out of this Country to finance Japan in a war against Russia. They created a reign of terror in Russia with our money in order to help that war along. They instigated the separate peace between Germany and Russia, and thus drove a wedge between the allies in World War. They financed Trotsky's passage from New York to Russia so that he might assist in the destruction of the Russian Empire. They fomented and instigated the Russian Revolution, and placed a large fund of American dollars at Trotsky's disposal in one of their branch banks in Sweden so that through him

Russian homes might be thoroughly broken up and Russian children flung far and wide from their natural protectors. They have since begun breaking up of American homes and the dispersal of American children. Mr. Chairman, there should be no partisanship in matters concerning banking and currency affairs in this Country, and I do not speak with any."

"In 1912 the National Monetary Association, under the chairmanship of the late Senator Nelson W. Aldrich, made a report and presented a vicious bill called the National Reserve Association bill. This bill is usually spoken of as the Aldrich bill. Senator Aldrich did not write the Aldrich bill. He was the tool, if not the accomplice, of the European bankers who for nearly twenty years had been scheming to set up a central bank in this Country and who in 1912 has spent and were continuing to spend vast sums of money to accomplish their purpose."

"We were opposed to the Aldrich plan for a central bank. The men who rule the Democratic Party then promised the people that if they were returned to power there would be no central bank established here while they held the reigns of government. Thirteen months later that promise was broken, and the Wilson administration, under the tutelage of those sinister Wall Street figures that stood behind Colonel House, established here in our free Country the worm-eaten monarchical institution of the "King's Bank" to control us from the top downward, and from the cradle to the grave. The Federal Reserve Bank

destroyed our old and characteristic way of doing business. It discriminated against our 1-name commercial paper, the finest in the world, and it set up the antiquated 2-name paper, which is the present curse of this Country and which wrecked every country which has ever given it scope; it fastened down upon the Country the very tyranny from which the framers of the Constitution sought to save us."

"One of the greatest battles for the preservation of this Republic was fought out here in Jackson's time; when the second Bank of the United States, founded on the same false principles of those which are here exemplified in the Fed was hurled out of existence. After that, in 1837, the Country was warned against the dangers that might ensue if the predatory interests after being cast out should come back in disguise and unite themselves to the Executive and through him acquire control of the Government. That is what the predatory interests did when they came back in the livery of hypocrisy and under false pretenses obtained the passage of the Fed. The danger that the Country was warned against came upon us and is shown in the long train of horrors attendant upon the affairs of the traitorous and dishonest Fed. Look around you when you leave this Chamber and you will see evidences of it in all sides. This is an era of misery and for the conditions that caused that miser; the Fed are fully liable. This is an era of financed crime and in the financing of crime the Fed does not play the part of a disinterested spectator. It has been said that the draughtsman who was employed to write the text of the Aldrich bill because that had been drawn up by lawyers, by acceptance bankers of European origin in New York. It was a copy, in general a translation of the statutes of the Reichsbank and other European central banks. One-half million dollars was spent on the part of the propaganda organized by these bankers for the purpose of misleading public opinion and giving Congress the impression that there was an overwhelming popular demand for it and the kind of currency that goes with it, namely, an asset currency based on human debts and obligations. Dr. H. Parker Willis had been employed by Wall Street and propagandists, and when the Aldrich measure failed- he obtained employment with Carter Glass, to assist in drawing the banking bill for the Wilson administration. He appropriated the text of the Aldrich bill. There is no secret about it. The text of the Federal Reserve Act was tainted from the first."

"Meanwhile and on account of it, we ourselves are in the midst of the greatest depression we have ever known. From the Atlantic to the Pacific, our Country has been ravaged and laid waste by the evil practices of the Fed and the interests which control them. At no time in our history, has the general welfare of the

people been at a lower level or the minds of the people so full of despair. Recently in one of our States, 60,000 dwelling houses and farms were brought under the hammer in a single day. 71,000 houses and farms in Oakland County, Michigan, were sold and their erstwhile owners dispossessed. The people who have thus been driven out are the wastage of the Fed. They are the victims of the Fed. Their children are the new slaves of the auction blocks in the revival of the institution of human slavery."

"In 1913, before the Senate Banking and Currency Committee, Mr. Alexander Lassen made the following statement: "The whole scheme of the Fed with its commercial paper is an impractical, cumbersome machinery- is simply a cover to secure the privilege of issuing money, and to evade payment of as much tax upon circulation as possible and then control the issue and maintain, instead of reducing interest rates. It will prove to the advantage of the few and the detriment of the people. It will mean continued shortage of actual money and further extension of credits, for when there is a shortage of money people have to borrow to their cost.' "A few days before the Fed passed, Senator Root denounced the Fed as an outrage on our liberties. He predicted: 'Long before we wake up from our dream of prosperity through an inflated currency, our gold- which alone could have kept us from catastrophe- will have vanished and no rate of interest will tempt it to return. If ever a prophecy came true, that one did. The Fed became law the day before Christmas Eve, in the year 1913, and shortly afterwards, the German International bankers, Kuhn, Loeb and Co. sent one of their partners here to run it."

"The Fed Note is essentially unsound. It is the worst currency and the most dangerous that this Country has ever known. When the proponents of the act saw that the Democratic doctrine would not permit them to let the proposed banks issue the new currency as bank notes, they should have stopped at that. They should not have foisted that kind of currency, namely, an asset currency, on the United States Government. They should not have made the Government debts of individuals and corporations, and, least of all, on the private debts of foreigners. As Kemerer says: 'The Fed Notes, therefore, in form, have some of the qualities of Government paper money, but in substance, are almost a pure asset currency possessing a Government guarantee against which contingency the Government has made no provision whatever. Hon. L.J.Hill, a former member of the House, said, and truly: 'They are obligations of the Government for which the United States received nothing and for the payment of which at any time, it assumes the responsibility: looking to the Fed to recoup itself. If this United States is to

redeem the Fed Notes, when the General Public finds it costs to deliver this paper to the Fed, and if the Government has made no provisions for redeeming them, the first element of unsoundness is not far to seek."

"Before the Banking and Currency Committee, when the bill was under discussion Mr. Crozier of Cincinnati said: 'The imperial power of elasticity of the public currency is wielded exclusively by the central corporations owned by the banks. This is a life and death power over all local banks and all business. It can be used to create or destroy prosperity, to ward off or cause stringencies and panics. By making money artificially scarce, interest rates throughout the Country can be arbitrarily raised and the bank tax on all business and cost of living increased for the profit of the banks owning these regional central banks, and without the slightest benefit to the people. The 12 Corporations together cover and monopolize and use for private gain- every dollar of the public currency and all public revenue of the United States. Not a dollar can be put into circulation among the people by their Government, without the consent of and on terms fixed by these 12 private money trusts. In defiance of this and all other warnings, the proponents of the Fed created the 12 private credit corporations and gave them an absolute monopoly of the currency of these United States- not of the Fed Notes alone- but of all other currency! The Fed Act providing ways and means by which the gold and general currency in the hands of the American people could be obtained by the Fed in exchange for Fed Notes- which are not money- but mere promises to pay. Since the evil day when this was done, the initial monopoly has been extended by vicious amendments to the Fed and by the unlawful and treasonable practices of the Fed."

"Mr. Chairman, if a Scottish distiller wishes to send a cargo of Scotch whiskey to these United States, he can draw his bill against the purchasing bootlegger in dollars and after the bootlegger has accepted it by writing his name across the face of it, the Scotch distiller can send that bill to the nefarious open discount market in New York City where the Fed will buy it and use it as collateral for a new issue of Fed Notes. Thus the Government of these United States pay the Scotch distiller for the whiskey before it is shipped, and if it is lost on the way, or if the Coast Guard seizes it and destroys it, the Fed simply write off the loss and the government never recovers the money that was paid to the Scotch distiller. While we are attempting to enforce prohibition here, the Fed are in the distillery business in Europe and paying bootlegger bills with public credit of these United States. Mr. Chairman, by the same process, they compel our Government to pay the German brewer for his beer. Why should the Fed be permitted to finance the *brewing industry in Germany either in this way or as they do by compelling small and fearful United States Banks to take stock in the Isenbeck Brewery and in the German Bank for brewing industries? Mr. Chairman, if Dynamit Nobel of Germany, wishes to sell dynamite in Japan to use in Manchuria or elsewhere, it can drew its bill against the Japanese customers in dollars and send that bill to the nefarious open discount market in New York City where the Fed will buy it and use it as collateral for a new issue of Fed Notes- while at the same time the Fed will be helping Dynamit Nobel by stuffing its stock into the United States banking system. Why should we send our representatives to the disarmament conference at Geneva- while the Fed is making our Government pay Japanese debts to German Munitions makers? Mr. Chairman, if a German wishes to raise a crop of beans and sell them to a Japanese customer, he can draw a bill against his prospective Japanese customer in dollars and have it purchased by the Fed and get the money out of this Country at the expense of the American people before he has even planted the beans in the ground. Mr. Chairman, if a German in Germany wishes to export goods to South America, or any other Country, he can draw his bill against his customers and send it to these United States and get the money out of this Country before he ships, or even manufactures the goods.*

Mr. Chairman, why should the currency of these United States be issued on the strength of German Beer? Why should it be issued on the crop of unplanted beans to be grown in Chili for Japanese consumption? Why should these United States be compelled to issue many billions of dollars every year to pay the debts of one foreigner to another foreigner? Was it for this that our National Bank depositors had their money taken out of our banks and shipped abroad? Was it for this that they had to lose it? Why should the public credit of these United States and likewise money belonging to our National Bank depositors be used to support foreign brewers, narcotic drug vendors, whiskey distillers, wig makers, human hair merchants, Chilean bean growers, to finance the munitions factories of Germany and Soviet Russia?"

"The United States has been ransacked and pillaged. Our structures have been gutted and only the walls are left standing. While being perpetrated, everything the world would rake up to sell us was brought in here at our expense by the Fed until our markets were swamped with unneeded and unwanted imported goods priced far above their value and make to equal the dollar volume of our honest exports, and to kill or reduce our favorite balance of trade. As Agents of the foreign central banks, the Fed try by every means in their power to reduce our

favorable balance of trade. They act for their foreign principal and they accept fees from foreigners for acting against the best interests of these United States. Naturally there has been great competition among foreigners for the favors of the Fed."

"What we need to do is to send the reserves of our National Banks home to the people who earned and produced them and who still own them and to the banks which were compelled to surrender them to predatory interests. Mr. Chairman, there is nothing like the Fed pool of confiscated bank deposits in the world. It is a public trough of American wealth in which the foreigners claim rights, equal to or greater than Americans. The Fed are agents of the foreign central banks. They use our bank depositors' money for the benefit of their foreign principals. They barter the public credit of the United States Government and hire it to our foreigners at a profit to themselves. All this is done at the expense of the United States Government and at a sickening loss to the American people. Only our great wealth enabled us to stand the drain of it as long as we did. We need to destroy the Fed wherein our national reserves are impounded for the benefit of the foreigners. "We need to save America for Americans."

"Mr. Chairman, when you hold a $10.00 Fed Note in your hand, you are holding a piece of paper which sooner or later is going to cost the United States Government $10.00 in gold, unless the Government is obliged to go off the gold standard. It is based on limburger cheese or in cans purported to contain peas or horse meat, illicit drugs, bootleggers fancies, rags and bones from Soviet Russia, of which these United States imported over a million dollars worth last year, on wines whiskey, natural gas, goat and dog fur, garlic on the string, and Bombay ducks. If you like to have paper money- which is secured by such commodities- you have it in Fed Note. If you desire to obtain the thing of value upon which this paper currency is based, that is, the limburger cheese, the whiskey, the illicit drugs, or any of the other staples- you will have a very hard time finding them. Many of these worshipful commodities are in foreign Countries. Are you going to Germany to inspect her warehouses to see if the specified things of value are there? I think more, I do not think that you would find them there if you did go."

"On April 27, 1932, the Fed outfit sent $750,000 belonging to American bank depositors in gold to Germany. A week later another $300,000 in gold was shipped to Germany. About the middle of May $12,000,000 in gold was shipped to Germany by the Fed. Almost every week there is a shipment of gold to

54

Germany. These shipments are not made for profit on the exchange since the German marks are below parity with the dollar. Mr. Chairman, I believe that the National Bank depositors of these United States have a right to know what the Fed is doing with their money. There are millions of National Bank depositors in the Country who do not know that a percentage of every dollar they deposit in a Member Bank of the Fed goes automatically to American Agents of the foreign banks and that all their deposits can be paid away to foreigners without their knowledge or consent by the crooked machinery of the Fed and the questionable practices of the Fed. Mr. Chairman, the American people should be told the truth by their servants in office. In 1930, we had over a half billion dollars outstanding daily to finance foreign goods stored in or shipped between several billion dollars. What goods are these on which the Fed yearly pledged several billions of dollars? In its yearly total, this item amounts to several billions of dollars of the public credit of these United States?"

"What goods are those which are hidden in European and Asiatic stores have not been seen by any officer of our Government but which are being financed on the public credit of the United States Government? What goods are those upon which the United States Government is being obligated by the Fed to issue Fed Notes to the extent of several billions of dollars a year? The Fed had been International Banks from the beginning, with these United States as their enforced banker and supplier of currency. But it is none the less extraordinary to see these twelve private credit monopolies, buying the debts of foreigners against foreigners, in all parts of the world and asking the Government of these United States for new issues of Fed notes in exchange for them. The magnitude of the acceptance racket as it has been developed by the Fed, their foreign correspondents, and the predatory European born bankers, who set up the Fed here and taught your own, by and of pirates, how to loot the people: 'I say the magnitude of this racket is estimated to be in the neighborhood of 9,000,000,000 per year. In the past ten years it is said to have amounted to $90,000,000,000.00.' In my opinion it has amounted to several times that much. Coupled to this you have to the extent of billions of dollars, the gambling in the United States securities, which takes place in the same open discount market- a gambling on which the Fed is now spending $100,000,000.00 per week."

"Fed Notes are taken from the U.S. Government in unlimited quantities. Is strange that the burden of supplying these immense sums of money to the gambling fraternity has at last proved too heavy for the American people to endure? Would it not be a national calamity to again bind down this burden on

the backs of the American people and by means of a long rawhide whip of the credit masters, compel them to enter another seventeen years of slavery? They are trying to do that now. They are trying to take $100,000,000.00 of the public credit of the United States every week, in addition to all their other seizures and they are sending that money to the nefarious open market in a desperate gamble to reestablish their graft as a going concern. They are putting the United States Government in debt to the extent of $100,000,000 a week, and with the money they are buying our Government securities for themselves and their foreign principals. Our people are disgusted with the experiences of the Fed. The Fed is not producing a loaf of bread, a yard of cloth, a bushel of corn, or a pile of cordwood by its check-kiting operations in the money market."

"Mr. Speaker, on the 13th of January of this year I addressed the House on the subject of the Reconstruction Finance Corporation. In the course of my remarks I made the following statement: In 1928 the member banks of the Fed borrowed $60,598,690,000 from the Fed on their fifteen-day promissory notes. Think of it. Sixty billion dollars payable on demand in gold in the course of one single year. The actual amount of such obligations called for six times as much monetary gold as there is in the world. Such transactions represent a grant in the course of one single years of about $7,000,000 to every member of the Fed. Is it any wonder that American labor which ultimately pays the cost of all banking operations of this Country has at last proved unequal to the task of supplying this huge total of cash and credit for the benefit of the stock market manipulators and foreign swindlers? In 1933 the Fed presented the staggering amount of $60,598,690,000 to its member banks at the expense of the wage earners and tax payers of these United States. In 1929, the year of the stock market crash, the Fed advanced $58,000,000,000 to member banks. In 1930 while the speculating banks were getting out of the stock market at the expense of the general public, the Fed advanced them $13,022,782,000. This shows that when the banks were gambling on the public credit of these United States as represented by the Fed currency they were subsidized to any amount they required by the Fed. When the swindle began to fall, the bankers knew it in advance and withdrew from the market. They got out with whole skins- and left the people of these United States to pay the piper. "My friend from Kansas, Mr. McGugin, has stated that he thought the Fed lent money on rediscounting. So they do, but they lend comparatively little that way. The real discounting that they do has been called a mere penny in the slot business. It is too slow for genuine high flyers. They discourage it. They prefer to subsidize their favorite banks by making them

56

$60,000,000,000 advances and they prefer to acquire assistance in the notorious open discount market in New York, where they can use it to control the price of stocks and bonds on the exchanges. For every dollar they advanced on discounts in 1928, they lent $33.00 to their favorite banks for whom they do a business of several billion dollars income tax on their profits to these United States. This is the John Law swindle over again. The theft of Teapot Dome was trifling compared to it. What King ever robbed his subject to such an extent as the Fed has robbed us? Is it any wonder that there have been lately ninety cases of starvation in one of the New York hospitals? Is there any wonder that the children are being abandoned?"

"The government and the people of these United States have been swindled by swindlers deluxe to whom the acquisition of American or a parcel of Fed Notes presented no more difficulty than the drawing up of a worthless acceptance in a Country not subject to the laws of these United States, by sharpers not subject to the jurisdiction of these United States, sharpers with strong banking "fence" on this side of the water, a "fence" acting as a receiver of a worthless paper coming from abroad, endorsing it and getting the currency out of the Fed for it as quickly as possible exchanging that currency for gold and in turn transmitting the gold to its foreign confederates. Such were the exploits of Ivar Krueger, Mr. Hoover's friend, and his rotten Wall Street bankers. Every dollar of the billions Kreuger and his gang drew out of this Country on acceptances was drawn from the government and the people of the United States through the Fed. The credit of the United States Government was peddled to him by the Fed for their own private gain. That is what the Fed has been doing for many years."

"They have been peddling the credit of this Government to the swindlers and speculators of all nations. That is what happens when a Country forsakes its Constitution and gives its sovereignty over the public currency to private interests. Give them the flag and they will sell it."

The nature of Kreuger's organized swindle and the bankrupt condition of Kreuger's combine was known here last June when Hoover sought to exempt Krueger's loan to Germany of $125,000,000 from the operation of the Hoover Moratorium. The bankrupt condition of Krueger's swindle was known her last summer when $30,000,000 was taken from the American taxpayers by certain bankers in New York for the ostensible purpose of permitting Krueger to make a loan to Colombia. Colombia never saw that money. The nature of Krueger's swindle was known here in January when he visited his friend, Mr. Hoover, at *the White House. It was known here in March before he went to Paris and committed suicide. Mr. Chairman, I think the people of the United States are entitled to know how many billions of dollars were placed at the disposal of Krueger and his gigantic combine by the Fed, and to know how much of our Government currency was issued and lost in the financing of that great swindle in the years during which the Fed took care of Krueger's requirements."*

"A few days ago, the President of the United States with a white face and shaking hands, went before the Senate of behalf of the moneyed interests and asked the Senate to levy a tax on the people so that foreigners might know that these United States would pay its debt to them. Most Americans thought it was the other way around. What does these United States owe foreigners? When and by whom was the debt incurred? It was incurred by the Fed, when they peddled the signature of the Government to foreigners- for a price. It is what the United States Government has to pay to redeem the obligations of the Fed. Thieves Go Scot Free! Are you going to let these thieves get off scot free? Is there one law for the looter who drives up to the door of the United States Treasury in his limousine and another for the United States Veterans who are sleeping on the floor of a dilapidated house on the outskirts of Washington?"

"The Baltimore and Ohio Railroad is here asking for a large loan from the people, and the wage earners and the taxpayers of these United States. It is begging for a handout from the Government. It is standing, cap in hand, at the door of the R.F.C. where all the jackals have gathered to the feast. It is asking for money that was raised from the people by taxation and wants this money of the poor for the benefit of Kuhn, Loeb and Co., the German International Bankers. Is there one law for the Baltimore and Ohio Railroad and another for the hungry veterans it threw off its freight cars the other day? Is there one law for sleek and prosperous swindlers who call themselves bankers and another law for the soldiers who defended the flag? The R.F.C. is taking over these worthless securities from the Investment Trusts with United States Treasury money at the expense of the American taxpayer and the wage earner. It will take twenty years to redeem our Government. Twenty years of penal servitude to pay off the gambling debts of the traitorous Fed and to vast flood of American wages and savings, bank deposits, and the United States Government credit which the Fed exported out of this country to their foreign principals."

"The Fed lately conducted an anti-hoarding campaign here. They took that extra money which they had persuaded the American people to put into the banks- they

58

sent it to Europe- along with the rest. In the last several months, they have sent $1,300,000,000 in gold to their foreign employers, their foreign masters, and every dollar of that gold belonged to the people of these United States and was unlawfully taken from them."

"Mr. Chairman, within the limits of the time allowed me, I cannot enter into a particularized discussion of the Fed. I have singled out the Fed currency for a few remarks because there has lately been some talk here of "fiat money". What kind of money is being pumped into the open discount market and through it into foreign channels and stock exchanges? Mr. Mills of the Treasury has spoken here of his horror of the printing presses and his horror of dishonest money. He has no horror of dishonest money. If he had, he would be no party to the present gambling of the Fed in the nefarious open discount market of New York, a market in which the sellers are represented by 10 discount corporations owned and organized by the very banks which own and control the Fed. What Mr. Mills is fighting for is the preservation, whole and entire, of the banker's monopoly of all the currency of the United States Government."

"Mr. Chairman, last December, I introduced a resolution here asking for an examination and an audit of the Fed and all related matters. If the House sees fit to make such an investigation, the people of these United States will obtain information of great value. This is a Government of the people, by the people, for the people. Consequently, nothing should be concealed from the people. The man who deceives the people is a traitor to these United States. The man who knows or suspects that a crime has been committed and who conceals and covers up that crime is an accessory to it. Mr. Speaker, it is a monstrous thing for this great nation of people to have its destinies presided over by a traitorous government board acting in secret concert with international usurers. Every effort has been made by the Fed to conceal its powers- but the truth is- the Fed has usurped the Government. It controls everything here and it controls all of our foreign relations. It makes and breaks governments at will."

"No man and no body of men are more entrenched in power than the arrogant credit monopoly which operated the Fed. What National Government has permitted the Fed to steal from the people should now be restored to the people. The people have a valid claim against the Fed. If that claim is enforced the Americans will not need to stand in the bread line, or to suffer and die of starvation in the streets. Women will be saved, families will be kept together, and American children will not be dispersed and abandoned."

"Here is a Fed Note. Immense numbers of the notes are now held abroad. I am told that they amount to upwards of a billion dollars. They constitute a claim against our Government and likewise a claim against our peoples' money to the extent of $1,300,000,000 which has within the last few months been shipped abroad to redeem Fed Notes and to pay other gambling debts of the traitorous Fed. The greater part of our money stock has been shipped to other lands. Why should we promise to pay the debts of foreigners to foreigners? Why should the Fed be permitted to finance our competitors in all parts of the world? Do you know why the tariff was raised? It was raised to shut out the flood of Fed Goods pouring in here from every quarter of the globe- cheap goods, produced by cheaply paid foreign labor, on unlimited supplies of money and credit sent out of this Country by the dishonest and unscrupulous Fed." The Fed is spending $100,000,000 a week buying government securities in the open market and are making a great bid for foreign business. They are trying to make rates so attractive that the human hair merchants and the distillers and other business entities in foreign land will come her and hire more of the public credit of the United States Government to pay the Fed outfit for getting it for them."

"Mr. Chairman, when the Fed was passed, the people of these United States did not perceive that a world system was being set up here which would make the savings of the American school teacher available to a narcotic-drug vendor in Acapulco. They did not perceive that these United States was to be lowered to the position of a coolie country which has nothing but raw material and heart, that Russia was destined to supply the man power and that this country was to supply the financial power to an "international superstate". A superstate controlled by international bankers, and international industrialists acting together to enslave the world for their own pleasure?"

"The people of these United States are being greatly wronged. They have been driven from their employments. They have been dispossessed from their homes. They have been evicted from their rented quarters. They have lost their children. They have been left to suffer and die for lack of shelter, food, clothing and medicine. The wealth of these United States and the working capital have been taken away from them and has either been locked in the vaults of certain banks and the great corporations or exported to foreign countries for the benefit of the foreign customers of these banks and corporations. So far as the people of the United States are concerned, the cupboard is bare. It is true that the warehouses and coal yards and grain elevators are full, but these are padlocked, and the *great banks and corporations hold the keys. The sack of these United States by the Fed is the greatest crime in history."*

"Mr. Chairman, a serious situation confronts the House of Representatives today. We are trustees of the people and the rights of the people are being taken away from them. Through the Fed the people are losing the rights guaranteed to them by the Constitution. Their property has been taken from them without due process of law. Mr. Chairman, common decency requires us to examine the public accounts of the Government and see what crimes against the public welfare have been committed. What is needed here is a return to the Constitution of these United States. The old struggle that was fought out here in Jackson's time must be fought our over again. The independent United States Treasury should be reestablished and the Government should keep its own money under lock and key in the building the people provided for that purpose."

"Asset currency, the devise of the swindler, should be done away with. The Fed should be abolished and the State boundaries should be respected. Bank reserves should be kept within the boundaries of the States whose people own them, and this reserve money of the people should be protected so that the International Bankers and acceptance bankers and discount dealers cannot draw it away from them. The Fed should be repealed, and the Fed Banks, having violated their charters, should be liquidated immediately. Faithless Government officials who have violated their oaths of office should be impeached and brought to trial. Unless this is done by us, I predict, that the American people, outraged, pillaged, insulted and betrayed as they are in their own land, will rise in their wrath, and will sweep the money changers out of the temple."

"Mr. Chairman, the United States is bankrupt: It has been bankrupted by the corrupt and dishonest Fed. It has repudiated its debts to its own citizens. Its chief foreign creditor is Great Britain, and a British bailiff has been at the White House and the British Agents are in the United States Treasury making inventory arranging terms of liquidations! Mr. Chairman, the Fed has offered to collect the British claims in full from the American public by trickery and corruption, if Great Britain will help to conceal its crimes. The British are shielding their agents, the Fed, because they do not wish that system of robbery to be destroyed here. They wish it to continue for their benefit! By means of it, Great Britain has become the financial mistress of the world. She has regained the position she occupied before the World War. For several years she has been a silent partner in the business of the Fed. Under threat of blackmail, or by their bribery, or by

61

their native treachery to the people of the United States, the officials in charge of the Fed unwisely gave Great Britain immense gold loans running into hundreds of millions of dollars. They did this against the law! Those gold loans were not single transactions. They gave Great Britain a borrowing power in the United States of billions. She squeezed billions out of this Country by means of her control of the Fed. As soon as the Hoover Moratorium was announced, Great Britain moved to consolidate her gains. After the treacherous signing away of American rights at the 7-power conference at London in July, 1931, which put the Fed under the control of the Bank of International Settlements, Great Britain began to tighten the hangman's noose around the neck of the United States. She abandoned the gold standard and embarked on a campaign of buying up the claims of foreigners against the Fed in all parts of the world. She has now sent her bailiff, Ramsey MacDonald, here to get her war debt to this country canceled. But she has a club in her hands! She has title to the gambling debts which the corrupt and dishonest Fed incurred abroad."

"Ramsey MacDonald, the labor party deserter, has come here to compel the President to sign on the dotted line, and that is what Roosevelt is about to do! Roosevelt will endeavor to conceal the nature of his action from the American people. But he will obey the International Bankers and transfer the war debt that Great Britain should pay to the American people, to the shoulders of the American taxpayers.

Mr. Chairman, the bank holiday in the several States was brought about by the corrupt and dishonest Fed. These institutions manipulated money and credit, and caused the States to order bank holidays. These holidays were frame-ups! They were dress rehearsals for the national bank holiday which Franklin D. Roosevelt promised Sir Ramsey MacDonald that he would declare. There was no national emergency here when Franklin D. Roosevelt took office excepting the bankruptcy of the Fed- a bankruptcy which has been going on under cover for several years and which has been concealed from the people so that the people would continue to permit their bank deposits and their bank reserves and their gold and the funds of the United States Treasury to be impounded in these bankrupt institutions. Under cover, the predatory International Bankers have been stealthily transferring the burden of the Fed debts to the people's Treasury and to the people themselves. They the farms and the homes of the United States to pay for their thievery! That is the only national emergency that there has been here since the depression began."

"The week before the bank holiday was declared in New York State, the deposits in the New York savings banks were greater than the withdrawals. There were no runs on New York Banks. There was no need of a banking holiday in New York or of a national holiday. Roosevelt did what the International Bankers ordered him to do! Do not deceive yourself, Mr. Chairman, or permit yourself to be deceived by others into the belief that Roosevelt's dictatorship is in any way intended to benefit the people of the United States: he is preparing to sign on the dotted line! He is preparing to cancel the war debts by fraud! He is preparing to internationalize this Country and to destroy our Constitution itself in order to keep the Fed intact as a money institution for foreigners. Mr. Chairman, I see no reason why citizens of the United States should be terrorized into surrendering their property to the International Bankers who own and control the Fed. The statement that gold would be taken from its lawful owners if they did not voluntarily surrender it, to private interests, show that there is an anarchist in our Government. The statement that it is necessary for the people to give their gold- the only real money- to the banks in order to protect the currency is a statement of calculated dishonesty! By his unlawful usurpation of power on the night of March 5, 1933, and by his proclamation, which in my opinion was in violation of the Constitution of the United States, Roosevelt divorced the currency of the United States from gold, and the United States currency is no longer protected by gold. It is therefore sheer dishonesty to say that the people's gold is needed to protect the currency. Roosevelt ordered the people to give their gold to private interests, that is, to banks, and he took control of the banks so that all the gold and gold values in them, or given into them, might be handed over to the predatory International Bankers who own and control the Fed. Roosevelt cast his lot with the usurers. He agreed to save the corrupt and dishonest at the expense of the people of the United States. He took advantage of the people's confusion and weariness and spread the dragnet over the United States to capture everything of value that was left in it. He made a great haul for the International Bankers."

"The Prime Minister of England came here for money! He came here to collect cash! He came here with Fed Currency and other claims against the Fed which England had bought up in all parts of the world. And he has presented them for redemption in gold. Mr. Chairman, I am in favor of compelling the Fed to pay their debts. I see no reason why the general public should be forced to pay the gambling debts of the International Bankers. By his action in closing the banks of the United States, Roosevelt seized the gold value of forty billions or more of bank deposits in the United States banks. Those deposits were deposits of gold

values. By his action he has rendered them payable to the depositors in paper only, if payable at all, and the paper money he proposes to pay out to bank depositors and to the people generally in lieu of their hard earned gold values in itself, and being based on nothing into which the people can convert it the said paper money is of negligible value altogether. It is the money of slaves, not of free men. If the people of the United States permit it to be imposed upon them at the will of their credit masters, the next step in their downward progress will be their acceptance of orders on company stores for what they eat and wear. Their case will be similar to that of starving coal miners. They, too, will be paid with orders on Company stores for food and clothing, both of indifferent quality and be forced to live in Company-owned houses from which they may be evicted at the drop of a hat. More of them will be forced into conscript labor camps under supervision."

"At noon on the 4th of March, 1933, FDR with his hand on the Bible took an oath to preserve, protect and defend the Constitution of the U.S. At midnight on the 5th of March, 1933, he confiscated the property of American citizens. He took the currency of the United States standard of value. He repudiated the internal debt of the Government to its own citizens. He destroyed the value of the American dollar. He released, or endeavored to release, the Fed from their contractual liability to redeem Fed currency in gold or lawful money on parity with gold. He depreciated the value of the national currency. The people of the U.S. are now using unredeemable paper slips for money. The Treasury cannot redeem that paper in gold or silver. The gold and silver of the Treasury has unlawfully been given to the corrupt and dishonest Fed. And the Administration has since had the effrontery to raid the country for more gold for the private interests by telling our patriotic citizens that their gold is needed to protect the currency. It is not being used to protect the currency! It is being used to protect the corrupt and dishonest Fed. The directors of these institutions have committed criminal offense against the United States Government, including the offense of making false entries on their books, and the still more serious offense of unlawfully abstracting funds from the United States Treasury! Roosevelt's gold raid is intended to help them out of the pit they dug for themselves when they gambled away the wealth and savings of the American people."

"The International Bankers set up a dictatorship here because they wanted a dictator who would protect them. They wanted a dictator who would issue a proclamation giving the Fed an absolute and unconditional release from their special currency in gold or lawful money of any Fed Bank."

64

"Has Roosevelt relieved any other class of debtors in this country from the necessity of paying their debts? Has he made a proclamation telling the farmers that they need not pay their mortgages? Has he made a proclamation to the effect that mothers of starving children need not pay their milk bills? Has he made a proclamation relieving householders from the necessity of paying rent? Not he! He has issued one kind of proclamation only, and that is a proclamation to relieve international bankers and the foreign debtors of the United States Government."

"Mr. Chairman, the gold in the banks of this country belongs to the American people who have paper money contracts for it in the form of national currency. If the Fed cannot keep their contracts with United States citizens to redeem their paper money in gold or lawful money, then the Fed must be taken over by the United States Government and their officers must be put on trial. There must be a day of reckoning. If the Fed looted the Treasury so that the Treasury cannot redeem the United States currency for which it is liable in gold, then the Fed must be driven out of the Treasury."

"Mr. Chairman, a gold certificate is a warehouse receipt for gold in the Treasury, and the man who has a gold certificate is the actual owner of a corresponding amount of gold stacked in the Treasury subject to his order. Now can Roosevelt, who seeks to render the money of the United States worthless by unlawfully declaring that it may, no longer be converted into gold at the will of the holder. Roosevelt's next haul for the International Bankers was the reduction in the pay of all Federal employees. Next in order are the veterans of all wars, many of whom are aged and inform, and other sick and disabled. These men had their lives adjusted for them by acts of Congress determining the amounts of the pensions, and, while it is meant that every citizen should sacrifice himself for the good of the United States, I see no reason why those poor people, these aged Civil War Veterans and war widows and half-starved veterans of the World War, should be compelled to give up their pensions for the financial benefit of the International vultures who have looted the Treasury, bankrupted the country and traitorously delivered the United States to a foreign foe."

"There are many ways of raising revenue that are better than that barbaric act of injustice. Why not collect from the Fed the amount they owe the U.S. Treasury in interest on all the Fed currency they have taken from the Government? That would put billions of dollars into the U.S. Treasury. If FDR is as honest as he pretends to be, he will have that done immediately. And in addition, why not

compel the Fed to disclose their profits and to pay the Government its share? Until this is done, it is rank dishonesty to talk of maintaining the credit of the U.S. Government. My own salary as a member of Congress has been reduced, and while I am willing to give my part of it that has been taken away from me to the U.S. Government, I regret that the U.S. has suffered itself to be brought so low by the vultures and crooks who are operating the roulette wheels and faro tables in the Fed, that is now obliged to throw itself on the mercy of its legislators and charwomen, its clerks, and it poor pensioners and to take money out of our pockets to make good the defalcations of the International Bankers who were placed in control of the Treasury and given the monopoly of U.S. Currency by the misbegotten Fed. I am well aware that the International Bankers, who drive up to the door of the United States Treasury in their limousines, look down with scorn upon members of Congress because we work for so little, while they draw millions a year. The difference is that we earn, or try to earn, what we get- and they steal the greater part of their takings. I do not like to see vivisections performed on human beings. I do not like to see the American people used for experimental purposes by the credit masters of the United States. They predicted among themselves that they would be able to produce a condition here in which American citizens would be completely humbled and left starving and penniless in the streets."

"The fact that they made the assertion while they were fomenting their conspiracy against the United States that they like to see a human being, especially an American, stumbling from hunger when he walks. Something should be done about it, they say. Five-cent meals or something! But FDR will not permit the House of Representatives to investigate the condition of the Fed. FDR will not do that. He has certain International Bankers to serve. They look to him as the man higher up who will protect them from the just wrath of an outraged people. The International Bankers have always hated our pensioners. A man with a small pension is a ward of the Government. He is not dependent upon them for a salary or wages. They cannot control him. They do not like him. It gave them great pleasure, therefore, to slash the veterans. But FDR will never do anything to embarrass his financial supporters. He will cover up the crimes of the Fed."

"Before he was elected, Mr. Roosevelt advocated a return to the earlier practices of the Fed, thus admitting its corruptness. The Democratic platform advocated a change in the personnel of the Fed. These were campaign bait. As a prominent

Democrat lately remarked to me; there is no new deal. The same old crowd is in control."

"The claims of foreign creditors of the Fed have no validity in law. The foreign creditors were the receivers- and the willing receivers- of stolen goods! They have received through their banking fences immense amounts of currency, and that currency was unlawfully taken from the United States Treasury by the Fed. England discovered the irregularities of the Fed quite early in its operations and through fear, apparently, the Fed have for years suffered themselves to be blackmailed and dragooned permitting England to share in the business of the Fed. The Fed have unlawfully taken many millions of dollars of the public credit of the United States and have given it to foreign sellers on the security of the debt paper of foreign buyers in purely foreign transactions, and when the foreign buyers refused to meet their obligations and the Fed saw no honest way of getting the stolen goods back into their possession, they decided by control of the executive to make the American people pay their losses! They likewise entered into a conspiracy to deprive the people of the U.S. of their title to the war debts and not being able to do that in the way they intended, they are now engaged in an effort to debase the American dollar so that foreign governments will have their debts to this country cut in two, and then by means of other vicious underhanded arrangements, they propose to remit the remainder."

"So far as the U.S. is concerned, the gambling counters have no legal standing. The U.S. Treasury cannot be compelled to make good the gambling ventures of the corrupt and dishonest Fed. Still less should the bank deposits of the U.S. be used for that purpose. Still less should the national currency have been made irredeemable in gold so that the gold which was massed and stored to redeem the currency for American citizens may be used to pay the gambling debts of the Fed for England's benefit. The American people should have their gold in their own possession where it cannot be held under secret agreement for any foreign control bank, or worldbank, or foreign nation. Our own citizens have the prior claim to it. The paper money men have in their possession deserves redemption far more than U.S. currency and credit which was stolen from the U.S. Treasury and bootlegged abroad."

"Why should the foreigners be made preferred creditors of the bankrupt U.S.? Why should the U.S. be treated as bankrupt at all? This Government has immense sums due it from the Fed. The directors of these institutions are men of great wealth. Why should the guilty escape the consequences of their misdeeds?

Why should the people of these U.S. surrender the value of their gold bank deposits to pay off the gambling debts of these bankers? Why should Roosevelt promise foreigners that the U.S. will play the part of a good neighbor, 'meeting its obligations'? Let the Fed meet their obligations. Every member of the Fed should be compelled to disgorge, and every acceptance banker and every discount corporation which has made illegal profits by means of public credit unlawfully bootlegged out of the U.S. Treasury and hired out by the crooks and vultures of the Fed should be compelled to disgorge. Gambling debts due to foreign receivers of stolen goods should not be paid by sacrificing our title to our war debts, the assets of the U.S. Treasury- which belong to all the people of the U.S. and which it is our duty to preserve inviolate in the people's treasury. The U.S. Treasury cannot be made liable for them. The Fed currency must be redeemed by the Fed banks or else these Fed banks must be liquidated."

"We know from assertions made here by the Hon. John N. Garner, Vice-President of the U.S. that there is a condition in the United States such would cause American citizens, if they knew what it was, to lose all confidence in their government. That is a condition that Roosevelt will not have investigated. He has brought with him from Wall Street, James Warburg, the son of Paul M. Warburg. Mr. Warburg, alien born, and the son of an alien who did not become naturalized here until several years after this Warburg's birth, is a son of a former partner of Kuhn, Loeb and Co., a grandson of another partner, a nephew of a former partner, and a nephew of a present partner. He holds no office in our Government, but I am told that he is in daily attendance at the Treasury, and that he has private quarters there! In other words, Mr. Chairman, Kuhn, Loeb & Company now has control and occupies the U.S. Treasury."

"The text of the Executive order which seems to place an embargo on shipments of gold permits the Secretary of the Treasury, a former director of the corrupt, to issue licenses at his discretion for the export of gold coin, or bullion, earmarked or held in trust for a recognized foreign government or foreign central bank for international settlement. Now, Mr. Chairman, if gold held in trust for those foreign institutions may be sent to them, I see no reason why gold held in trust for American as evidenced by their gold certificates and other currency issued by the U.S. Government should not be paid to them. I think that American citizens should be entitled to treatment at least as good as that which the person is extending to foreign governments, foreign central banks, and the bank of International Settlements. I think a veteran of the world war, with a $20.00 gold certificate, is at least as much entitled to receive his own gold for it, as any

international banker in the city of New York or London. By the terms of this executive order, gold may be exported if it is actually required, for the fulfillment of any contract entered into prior to the date of this order by an applicant who, in obedience to the executive order of April 5, 1933, has delivered gold coin, gold bullion, or gold certificates. This means that gold may be exported to pay the obligations abroad of the Fed which were incurred prior to the date of the order, namely, April 20, 1933."

"If a European Bank should send 100,000,000 dollars in Fed currency to a bank in this country for redemption, that bank could easily ship gold to Europe in exchange for that currency. Such Fed currency would represent "contracts" entered into prior to the date of the order. If the Bank of International Settlements or any other foreign bank holding any of the present gambling debt paper of the Fed should draw a draft for the settlement of such obligation, gold would be shopped to them because the debt contract would have been entered into prior to the date of order."

"Mr. Speaker, I rise to a question of constitutional privilege. Whereas, I charge. . .Eugene Meyer, Roy A. Young, Edmund Platt, Eugene B. Black, Adolph Casper Miller, Charles S. Hamlin, George R. James, Andrew W. Mellon, Ogden L. Mills, William H. Woo W. Poole, J.F.T. O'Connor, members of the Federal Reserve Board; F. H. Curtis, J.H. Chane, R.L. Austin, George De Camp, L.B. Williams, W.W. Hoxton, Oscar Newton, E.M. Stevens, J.S. Wood, J.N. Payton, M.L. McClure, C.C. Walsh, Isaac B. Newton, Federal Reserve Agents, jointly and severally, with violations of the Constitution and laws of the United States, and whereas I charge them with having taken funds from the U.S Treasury which were not appropriated by the Congress of the United States, and I charge them with having unlawfully taken over $80,000,000,000 from the U.S. Government in the year 1928, the said unlawful taking consisting of the unlawful creation of claims against the U.S. Treasury to the extent of over $80,000,000,000 in the year 1928; and I charge them with similar thefts committed in 1929, 1930, 1931, 1932 and 1933, and in years previous to 1928, amounting to billions of dollars; and whereas I charge them, jointly and severally with having unlawfully created claims against the U.S. Treasury by unlawfully placing U.S. Government credit in specific amounts to the credit of foreign governments and foreign central banks of issue; private interests and commercial and private banks of the U.S. and foreign countries, and branches of foreign banks doing business in the U.S., to the extent of billions of dollars; and with having made unlawful contracts in the name of the U.S. Government and the U.S. Treasury; and with having made

false entries on books of account; and whereas I charge them jointly and severally, with having taken Fed Notes from the U.S. Treasury ensued Fed Notes and with having put Fed Notes into circulation without obeying the mandatory provision of the Fed Act which requires the Fed Board to fix an interest rate on all issues of Fed Notes supplied to Fed Banks, the interest resulting there from to be paid by the Fed Banks to the government of the U.S. for the use of the Fed Notes, and I charge them of having defrauded the U.S. Government and the people of the U.S. of billions of dollars by the commission of this crime, and whereas I charge them, jointly and severally, with having purchased U.S. Government securities with U.S. Government credit unlawfully taken and with having sold the said U.S. Government securities back to the people of the U.S. for gold or gold values and with having again purchased U.S. Government securities with U.S. Government credit unlawfully taken and with having again sold the said U.S. Government security for gold or gold values, and I charge them with having defrauded the U.S. Government and the people of the U.S. by this rotary process; and whereas I charge them, jointly and severally, with having unlawfully negotiated U.S. Government securities, upon which the Government liability was extinguished, as collateral security for Fed Notes and with having substituted such securities for gold which was being held as collateral security for Fed Notes, and with having by the process defrauded the U.S. Government and the people of the U.S., and I charge them with the theft of all the gold and currency they obtained by this process; and whereas I charge them, jointly and severally, with having unlawfully issued Fed currency on false, worthless and fictitious acceptances and other circulating evidence of debt, and with having made unlawful advances of Fed currency, and with having unlawfully permitted renewals of acceptances and renewals of other circulating evidences of debt, and with having permitted acceptance bankers and discount dealer corporations and other private bankers to violate the banking laws of the U.S.; and whereas I charge them, jointly and severally, with having conspired to have evidences of debt to the extent of $1,000,000,000 artificially created at the end of February, 1933, and early in March 1933, and with having made unlawful issues and advances of Fed currency on the security of said artificially created evidences of debt for a sinister purpose, and with having assisted in the execution of said sinister purpose; and whereas I charge them, jointly and severally, with having brought about the repudiation of the currency obligations of the Fed Banks to the people of the U.S. and with having conspired to obtain a release for the Fed Board and the Fed Banks from their contractual liability to redeem all Fed currency in gold or lawful money at the Fed Bank and with having defrauded the holders of Fed currency, and with having conspired to have the debts and losses

70

of the Fed Board and the Fed Banks unlawfully transferred to the Government and the people of the U.S., and whereas I charge them, jointly and severally, with having unlawfully substituted Fed currency and other irredeemable paper currency for gold in the hands of the people after the decision to repudiate the Fed currency and the national currency was made known to them, and with thus having obtained money under false pretenses; and whereas I charge them, jointly and severally, with having brought about a repudiation of the n of the U.S. in order that the gold value of the said currency might be given to private interests, foreign governments, foreign central banks of issues, and the Bank of International Settlements, and the people of the U.S. to be left without gold or lawful money and with no currency other that a paper currency irredeemable in gold, and I charge them with having done this for the benefit of private interests, foreign governments, foreign central banks of issue, and the bank of International Settlements; and whereas I charge them, jointly and severally, with conniving with the Edge Law banks, and other Edge Law institutions, accepting banks, and discount corporations, foreign central banks of issue, foreign commercial banks, foreign corporations, and foreign individuals with funds unlawfully taken from the U.S. Treasury; and I charge them with having unlawfully permitted and made possible 'new financing' for foreigners at the expense of the U.S. Treasury to the extent of billions of dollars and with having unlawfully permitted and made possible the bringing into the United States of immense quantities of foreign securities, created in foreign countries for export to the U.S. and with having unlawfully permitted the said foreign securities to be imported into the U.S. instead of gold, which was lawfully due to the U.S. on trade balances and otherwise, and with having lawfully permitted and facilitated the sale of the said foreign securities in the U.S., and whereas I charge them, jointly and severally, with having unlawfully exported U.S. coins and currency for a sinister purpose, and with having deprived the people of the U.S. of their lawful medium of exchange, and I charge them with having arbitrarily and unlawfully reduced the amount of money and currency in circulation in the U.S. to the lowest rate per capita in the history of the Government, so that the great mass of the people have been left without a sufficient medium of exchange, and I charge them with concealment and evasion in refusing to make known the amount of U.S. money in coins and paper currency exported and the amount remaining in the U.S. as a result of which refusal the Congress of the U.S. is unable to ascertain where the U.S. coins and issues of currency are at the present time, and what amount of U.S. currency is now held abroad; and whereas I charge them, jointly and severally, with having arbitrarily and unlawfully raised and lowered the rates of money and with having arbitrarily increased and diminished the volume of currency in circulation for the benefit of private interests at the expense of the Government and the people of the U.S. and with having unlawfully manipulated money rates, wages, salaries and property values both real and personal, in the U.S. by unlawful operations in the open discount market and by resale and repurchase agreements unsanctioned by law, and whereas I charge them jointly and severally, with having brought about the decline in prices on the New York Stock Exchange and other exchanges in October, 1929, by unlawful manipulation of money rates and the volume of U.S. money and currency in circulation: by theft of funds from the U.S. Treasury by gambling in acceptances and U.S. Government securities; by service rendered to foreign and domestic speculators and politicians, and by unlawful sale of U.S. gold reserves abroad, and whereas the unconstitutional inflation law imbedded in the so-called Farm Relief Act by which the Fed Banks are given permission to buy U.S. Government securities to the extent of $3,000,000,000 and to drew forth currency from the people's Treasury to the extent of $3,000,000,000 is likely to result in connivance on the part of said accused with others in the purchase by the Fed of the U.S. Government securities to the extent of $3,000,000,000 with U.S. Government's own credit unlawfully taken,-it being obvious that the Fed do no not intend to pay anything of value to the U.S. Government for the said U.S. Government securities no provision for payment in gold or lawful money appearing in the so-called Farm Relief bill- and the U.S. Government will thus be placed in a position of conferring a gift of $3,000,000,000 in the U.S. Government securities on the Fed to enable them to pay more on their bad debts to foreign governments, foreign central banks of issue, private interests, and private and commercial banks, both foreign and domestic, and the Bank of International Settlements, and whereas the U.S. Government will thus go into debt to the extent of $3,000,000,000 and will then have an additional claim of $3,000,000,000 in currency unlawfully created against it and whereas no private interest should be permitted to buy U.S. Government securities with the Government's own credit unlawfully taken and whereas currency should not be issued for the benefit of said private interest or any interests on U.S. Government securities so acquired, and whereas it has been publicly stated and not denied that the inflation amendment of the Farm Relief Act is the matter of benefit which was secured by Ramsey MacDonald, the Prime Minister of Great Britain, upon the occasion of his latest visit to the U.S. Treasury, and whereas there is grave danger that the accused will employ the provision creating U.S. Government securities to the extent of $3,000,000,000 and three millions in currency to be for the benefit of themselves and their foreign principals, and that they will convert the currency so obtained to the uses of Great Britain by secret arrangements with *the Bank of England of which they are the agents, and for which they maintain an account and perform services at the expense of the U.S. Treasury, and that they will likewise confer benefits upon the Bank of International Settlements for which they maintain an account and perform services at the expense of the U.S. Treasury; and whereas I charge them, jointly and severally, with having concealed the insolvency of the Fed and with having failed to report the insolvency of the Fed to the Congress and with having conspired to have the said insolvent institutions continue in operation, and with having permitted the said insolvent institutions to receive U.S. Government funds and other deposits, and with having permitted them to exercise control over the gold reserves of the U.S. and with having permitted them to transfer upward of $100,000,000,000 of their debts and losses to the general public and the Government of the U.S., and with having permitted foreign debts of the Fed to be paid with the property, the savings, the wages, and the salaries of the people of the U.S. and with the farms and the homes of the American people, and whereas I charge them with forcing the bad debts of the Fed upon the general public covertly and dishonestly and with taking the general wealth and savings of the people of the U.S. under false pretenses, to pay the debts of the Fed to foreigners; and whereas I charge them, jointly and severally, with violations of the Fed Act and other laws; with maladministration of the he vasions of the Fed Law and other laws; and with having unlawfully failed to report violations of law on the part of the Fed Banks which, if known, would have caused the Fed Banks to lose their charters, and whereas I charge them, jointly and severally, with failure to protect and maintain the gold reserves and the gold stock and gold coinage of the U.S. and with having sold the gold reserves of the U.S to foreign Governments, foreign central banks of issue, foreign commercial and private banks, and other foreign institutions and individuals at a profit to themselves, and I charge them with having sold gold reserves of the U.S. so that between 1924 and 1928 the U.S. gained no gold on net account but suffered a decline in its percentage of central gold reserves from the 45.9 percent in 1924 to 37.5 percent in 1928 notwithstanding the fact that the U.S. had a favorable balance of trade throughout that period, and whereas I charge them, jointly and severally, with having conspired to concentrate U.S. Government securities and thus the national debt of the U.S. in the hands of foreigners and international money lenders and with having conspired to transfer to foreigners and international money lenders title to and control of the financial resources of the U.S.; and whereas I charge them, jointly and severally, with having fictitiously paid installments on the national debt with Government credit unlawfully taken; and whereas I charge them, jointly and severally, with the loss of the U.S.*

Government funds entrusted to their care; and whereas I charge them, jointly and severally, with having destroyed independent banks in the U.S. and with having thereby caused losses amounting to billions of dollars to the said banks, and to the general public of the U.S., and whereas I charge them, jointly and severally, with the failure to furnish true reports of the business operations and the true conditions of the Fed to the Congress and the people, and having furnished false and misleading reports to the congress of the U.S., and whereas I charge them, jointly and severally, with having published false and misleading propaganda intended to deceive the American people and to cause the U.S. to lose its independence; and whereas I charge them, jointly and severally, with unlawfully allowing Great Britain to share in the profits of the Fed at the expense of the Government and the people of the U.S.; and whereas I charge them, jointly and severally, with having entered into secret agreements and illegal transactions with Montague Norman, Governor of the Bank of England; and whereas I charge them, jointly and severally, with swindling the U.S. Treasury and the people of the U.S. in pretending to have received payment from Great Britain of the amount due on the British war debt to the U.S. in December, 1932; and whereas I charge them, jointly and severally, with having conspired with their foreign principals and others to defraud the U.S. Government and to prevent the people of the U.S. from receiving payment of the war debts due to the U.S. from foreign nations; and whereas I charge them, jointly and severally, with having robbed the U.S Government and the people of the U.S. by their theft and sale of the gold reserves of the U.S. and other unlawful transactions created a deficit in the U.S. Treasury, which has necessitated to a large extent the destruction of our national defense and the reduction of the U.S. Army and the U.S. Navy and other branches of the national defense; and whereas I charge them, jointly and severally, of having reduced the U.S. from a first class power to one that is dependent, and with having reduced the U.S. from a rich and powerful nation to one that is internationally poor; and whereas I charge them, jointly and severally, with the crime of having treasonable conspired and acted against the peace and security of the U.S. and with having treasonable conspired to destroy constitutional Government in the U.S., District of Columbia or elsewhere, whether or not the House is sitting, has recessed or has adjourned, to hold such clerical, stenographic, and other assistants, to require of such witnesses and the production of such books, papers, and documents, to take such testimony, to have such printing and binding done, and to make such expenditures as it deems necessary."

Only days after Congressman MacFadden's condemnation of the Federal Reserve, two shots were fired at him from an unknown, would-be assassin as he exited a car and walked toward a Washington D. C. hotel. Then weeks later while attending a political banquet, MacFadden fell violently ill from what later was discovered poisoning. His life was spared by a physician attending the banquet, procuring a stomach pump and gave the Congressman emergency treatment. He would die in 1936 on a visit to New York City of sudden heart failure after being diagnosed with a suspicious intestinal ailment.

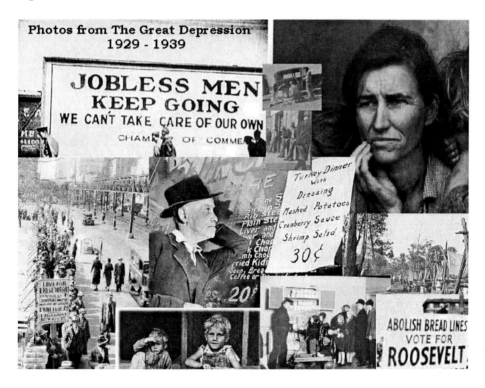

Photos from The Great Depression 1929 - 1939

Chapter VI
President Franklin D. Roosevelt vs. Big Business

The Great Depression!

The Federal Reserve's Capitalists Created It!
President Hoover Fueled It!

Roosevelt Cured It!

Hoover

Roosevelt

President Roosevelt escaped an assassination attempt days before taking office, then followed through on his campaign promises of change and regulate big business to protect the average citizen from capitalist's endless greed.

"The Federal Reserve definitely caused the Great Depression."

- Milton Friedman,
Nobel Prize winner in Economics

Since the time the elitist bankers of New York and Europe got control of the United States Federal Reserve in 1914, they treated the Federal Reserve Central Banking System as their own personal bank account. They received multi-million dollar low interest loans to increase the own financial and industrial empires. They also got huge low interest loans for foreign governments they would later use to influence. For foreign and domestic businesses, they would first indebt them, then bankrupt them with more loans and finally their own empire's institutions would take them over for pennies on the dollar. Irresponsible actions by the Federal Reserve of floating such huge loans on mostly speculation, the Federal Reserve's cash flow became limited to the degree in the late 1920s they were unable to do the job they were created to do, to halt "banking panics" and prevent "runs on local bank's cash flow" by providing cash and credit to those smaller American banks.

In 1923 Republican President Harding died and Vice-President Coolidge took office, which was the same year Congress' both houses were controlled by the Republican Party. Coolidge as President governed much the opposite as he did as Governor of Massachusetts when from 1919 to 1921 he supported child labor laws, labor hour and wages legislation, safety measures in factories and worker's representation on corporate boards. As President, Coolidge gave free reign to big business & corporations to run their empires as the seen fit while cutting their taxes. Such policies throughout his presidency during the "Roaring Twenties" diminish what little middleclass that existed and forcing workers to work for what was offered to them; which was barley enough to pay for food and rent. The combination of inflation, stagnated wages that gave the worker less buying power for their buck, tax cutting for big businesses and wealthy and irresponsible handling of Federal Reserve's money by its wealthy owners on speculation, fraud and corruption put the country into the "Great Depression." President Hoover followed with the same reckless policies during the first four years of the Great Depression and to his dieing day spoke out publicly against Roosevelt's "New Deal" and government aid policies.

It would be 72 years, from 1929 to 2001, before voters would ever allow the Republican Party to control all three branches of the United States government again. And like in the 1920s, the Republican Party from 2001 to 2006 would allow big business and financial institutions free reign on running their companies the way they wish. They deregulated financial institutions with little or no accountability that brought down the financial and industrial businesses to almost bankruptcy with an economic collapse that cost millions their jobs and tens of thousand of home foreclosures.

 "The decline of great powers is caused by simple economic over extension." *The Rise & Fall of Great Powers*
by Paul Kennedy

When Franklin Roosevelt became President in March of 1933, the United States was in the Greatest Depression of the country's history. Unemployment was at 25%, over one million was homeless, industrial production since 1929 fell 50% and farmer's goods prices fell 60%. The Federal Reserve System that was created to prevent such an "economic collapse" had failed because of the System's major stockholders mishandled the loans for their own empire's institutions and irresponsible speculation of markets foreign and domestic. In 32 of the 48 states that their banks were forced to become members of the Federal Reserve System, banks were closed because the Federal Reserve was unable to fulfill the obligation they promised; to provide their member banks with cash and loans needed in the spring of 1933. The Federal Reserve on March 5th was unable to open because they had squandered away hundreds of millions of dollars of the government and depositor's money on speculative loans both foreign and domestic and to enrich the stockholders empire's profits.

"Primarily this is because rulers of the exchange of mankind's goods have failed through their own stubbornness and their own incompetence, have admitted their

failure, and have abdicated. Practices of the unscrupulous money changers stand indicted in the court of public opinion, rejected by the hearts and minds of men. True they have tried, but their efforts have been cast in the pattern of an outworn tradition. Faced by failure of credit they have proposed only the lending of more money. Stripped of the lure of profit by which to induce our people to follow their false leadership, they have resorted to exhortations, pleading tearfully for restored confidence....The money changers have fled from their high seats in the temple of our civilization. We may now restore that temple to the ancient truths. The measure of the restoration lies in the extent to which we apply social values more noble than mere monetary profit." - President Roosevelt

President Roosevelt "New Deal"
Direct *relief,* Economic *recovery* and Financial *reform*

Getting food to people and getting them back to work was Roosevelt's first task. Immediate *relief* came to the most in need by way of Roosevelt expanding Hoover's Federal Emergency Relief Administration, (FERA), and to give direct assistance to the unemployed and their families. From May of 1933 to December of 1935, FERA provided over 20 million jobs under work relief programs Civilian Conservation Corp, (CCC), Public Works Administration, (PWA), and in 1935 added Works Progress Administration, (WPA). Most of FERA jobs were to build and repair public facilities and the country's infrastructure, such as airports, city halls, dams, highways, libraries, parks, recreational fields, sewers, streets and utilities. A small percentage of FERA money was allocated to art projects producing hundreds of thousands of pieces of art and concerts with audiences totaling well over 160 million.

The Great Depression was also caused by market instability caused by an embalance of power and information between the powerful stockholders of the Federal Reserve with their empires in industry and banking, and interests of farmers, labor, small businesses and the common depositor. During the 1920s, big business had the upper hand over its employees and unfairly used it for their higher profits. As unemployment increased, big business demanded more work for less pay. Labor had no recourse but to do as their employers demanded or lose their job.

Buckeye Steel Casting Company

A popular and unfair business practice in the 1920s was used by Samuel Bush, great-grandfather to G.W. Bush, and president of Buckeye Steel from 1908 to 1937. He would use the threat of replacing employees with unemployed-homeless people to force them to sometimes work 12 hour shiffs and 7 days a week.

Recovery came slow, but with each program passed by Congress with President Roosevelt's signature and exsisting programs expanded, progress was being made.

President Hoover's 1932 Reconstruction Finance Corporation, (RFC), aided states and local governments and made loans for home mortgages, to banks, railroads, farm mortgages, and other businesses was expanded by President Roosevelt.
The 1933 Agricultural Adjustment Act (or AAA), restricted production by paying farmers to reduce their crop area. Its purpose was to reduce crop surplus so as to effectively raise the value of crops, thereby giving farmers relative stability again. The farmers were paid subsidies by the federal government for leaving some of their fields unused. The Act created a new agency, the Agricultural Adjustment Administration, to oversee the distribution of the subsidies. It is considered the first modern U.S. farm bill.

National Industrial Recovery Act (NIRA) of 1933 was to *reform* the economy. It forced industries to come up with codes that established rules of operation for all firms within specific industries, such as minimum prices, agreements not to compete, and production restrictions while allowing the organization of unions. This Act big business was against and they took it to the United States Supreme Court where they deemed it unconstitutional in 1935.

In 1933, the Democat controlled Congress gave the Federal Trade Commission broad new regulatory powers to protect the consumer, eliminate anti-competitive business practices and enforce exsisting anti-monopoly and cartal laws that weren't being enforced. One such law not properly being enforced was the 1890 Sherman Antitrust Act that was passed to eliminate cartals and monopolies. "Every contract, combination in the form of trust or otherwise, or conspiracy, in restraint of trade or commerce among the several States, or with foreign nations, is declared to be illegal. That every person who shall monopolize, or attempt to monopolize, or combine or conspire with any other person or persons, to monopolize any part of the trade or commerce among the several States, or with foreign nations, shall be deemed guilty of a felony." The Act put responsibility upon government attorneys and district courts to pursue and investigate trusts, companies and organizations suspected of violating the Act. Another unforced law was the 1914 Clayton Act extended the right to sue under the antitrust laws to "any person who shall be injured in his business or property by reason of anything forbidden in the antitrust laws." Under the Clayton Act, private parties may bring suit in U.S. district court and should they prevail, they may be awarded treble damages and the cost of suit, including reasonable attorney's fees.

President Roosevelt's "New Deal" policies were working and unemployment fell from 25% to when he took office to 10% the day before America got into World War II.

President Roosevelt changes Wall Street, Securities & Investments like no other President before or since!

President Roosevelt appoints Joseph Kennedy Chairman of the United States Securities & Exchange Commission!

Chairman Joseph P. Kennedy, (middle with glasses)

Under Joe Kennedy's direction, the Securities & Exchange Commission enacted several major new banking regulations to protect the common depositor, the farmer and small businesses from the abuses they suffered at the hands of corporate empires. One was that a handfull of Wall Street's elitists would no longer have a monopoly on information they used to monipulate the markets or profit from insider trading. Wall Street's Exchange members were forced by law to make quarterly reports on their company's profits.

In 1934, President Roosevelt also leveled the playing field of investment on Wall Street. Although from 1911 to 1933 there were *"Blue Sky Laws"* adopted by all the states except Nevada to regulate the offering and sales of securities to protect the public from fraud, Investment Banking Association told its members as early as 1915 they could "ignore" the state enforced *"Blue Sky Laws."*

"It was a strikingly information-starved environment. Many firms whose securities were publicly traded published no regular reports or issued reports whose data were so arbitrarily selected and capriciously audited as to be worse than useless. It was this circumstance that had conferred such awesome power on a handful of investment bankers like J.P. Morgan, because they commanded a virtual monopoly of the information necessary for making sound financial decisions. Especially in the secondary markets, where reliable information was all but impossible for the average investor to come by, opportunities abounded for insider manipulation and wildcat speculation." - David Kennedy, author of *Freedom From Fear* describing "Wall Street" before the Securities Exchange Act of 1934

The Pecora Commission is the name commonly used to describe the commission established on March 4, 1932, by the United States Senate Committee on Banking, Housing, and Urban Affairs to investigate the causes of the Wall Street Crash of 1929. The Commission uncovered a wide range of abusive practices on the part of banks and bank affiliates. These included a variety of conflicts of interest such as the underwriting of unsound securities in order to pay off bad bank loans as well as "pool operations" to support the price of bank stocks. As a result of their findings came support for federal securities laws, the Security Act of 1933 and the Security Exchange Act of 1934. *Securities Act of 1933* required that investors receive significant information concerning securities being offered for public sale and prohibit deceit, misrepresentations, and other fraud in the sale of securities.

Securities Exchange Act of 1934 was legislation that expanded the regulations of the **Securities Act of 1933** as well added wide sweeping controls over securities in exchanges, associations and self-regulatory organizations. The Act also gave brokers and insurers guidelines of how they must conduct business, including the trillion dollar business of "secondary securities" trading by common people not within the close-knit Security Industry and Wall Street. Anti-fraud provisions were also added to protect the investor and catch the cheaters.

United States Securities and Exchange Commission (SEC), *June of 1934,* is a United States government agency having primary responsibility for enforcing the federal securities laws and regulating the securities industry/stock market. The main reason for the creation of the SEC was to regulate the stock market and prevent corporate abuses relating to the offering and sale of securities and corporate reporting.

Members of Wall Street Exchange would by law make public quarterly profit reports. **United States Trust Indenture Act of 1939** *(TIA),* supplements the Securities Act of 1933 in the case of the distribution of debt securities. Generally speaking, the TIA requires the appointment of a suitably independent and qualified trustee to act for the benefit of the holders of the securities, and specifies various substantive provisions for the trust indenture that must be entered into by the issuer and the trustee.

Investment Company Act of 1940 Specifically, the act regulated conflicts of interest in investment companies and securities exchanges. It protected the public primarily by legally requiring disclosure of material details about the investment company.

The Investment Advisers Act of 1940, is a United States federal law that was created to regulate the actions of investment advisers as defined by the law.

The National Labor Relations Act created a fairer balance between business and labor. No more could business threaten their workers of getting fired for not working overtime or seven days a week as most corporate companies would do before the Act was law. President Roosevelt changed the entire way corporations and companies delt with their employees, that is, until President Reagan stopped inforcing the *National Labor Relation Act* in the 1980s by allowing corporations and companies to "bust unions" by allowing management to replace any striking employees.

81

Chapter VII
Owner vs Labor Wars & President Harry S. Truman

With World War II ended, the industrialists returned to their "heavy handed" way of managing, negociating pay and conditions with their employees as if the Sherman Antitrust Law was never signed. Management would threaten their subordenants of being replaced by unemployed workers if they didn't work the hours requested of them for the pay they were offered and under the substandard conditions they were offering. Labor Union Management on the other hand were facing problems on two fronts. First, to indocrinate the fighting soldiers of World War II from the daily caous of war to a more consistant riggers of performing within the work place. Secondly, union management fought daily with company management for fairer pay, working conditions and resonable working hours. The worker were also facing problems on many fronts within their life including to adjusting to a new way of living after years surrounded by war and death. Although the average soldier was happy to be home among their families and love ones, being in the middle of labor wars just to be able to survive finacially and begin a new life as a non-fighting civilian would add a burden on them. The soldier, now civilian who had risked their life daily to win the freedoms the citizens of America was now enjoying, and while most industrialists were sitting comfortable at home making millions from the war machine, felt they deserve far more than what little management was offering. On the other hand, management was under the pressing thumb of their industrialist greedy owners that insisted on higher profits for themselves so that the could expand their empires from as cheap as possible labor force. To the idustrialists, the past was history and their only concern was to get as much profit as possible on the backs of labor, whether they are veterans of World War II or not. This ungratiful attitude of the industrialists force the common workers to turn to labor unions for representation to get a fair wage and better working conditions.

President Truman faced inflation as much as 6% in one month that was caused by greedy industrialists and destablizing labor strikes in several major industries. A parilizing railroad strike, unprecedented in the country's history, that stopped all passenger and consumer product's movement for over a month. After labor turned down a final proposal by the railroad's management, Truman lost favor with union members after he seeked power before Congress to seize control of the railroads and threatened to draft striking workers into the armed forces. But during the speech Truman received word that the railroad strike ended on his terms.

The Labor-Management Relations Act, commonly known as the Taft-Hartley Act, is a United States federal law that greatly restricts the activities and power of labor unions. Congress passed the pro-business law over President Truman's veto.

Taft-Hartly Act

To promote the full flow of commerce, to prescribe the legitimate rights of both employees and employers in their relations affecting commerce, to provide orderly and peaceful procedures for preventing the interference by either with the legitimate rights of the other, to protect the rights of individual employees in their relations with labor organizations whose activities affect commerce, to define and proscribe practices on the part of labor and management which affect commerce and are inimical to the general welfare, and to protect the rights of the public in connection with labor disputes affecting commerce.

"The Taft-Hartley Act is nothing less than the legalization for slave labor."

The 1951 Steel Strike

The 1952 steel strike was by the United Steel Workers of America against U.S. Steel and nine other steelmakers. The strike was scheduled to begin on April 9, 1952, but President Harry S. Truman nationalized the American steel industry hours before the workers walked out. The steel companies sued to regain control of their facilities. On June 2, 1952, in a landmark decision, the United States Supreme Court ruled in Youngstown Sheet & Tube Co. v. Sawyer, 343 U.S. 579 (1952), that the president lacked the authority to seize the steel mills. The Steelworkers struck to win a wage increase. The strike lasted 53 days, and ended on July 24, 1952, on essentially the same terms the union had proposed four months earlier. Through the 1950's, labor union and middleclass labor enjoyed great amount of expantion while big business also enjoyed profits while being held in check both by unions and government laws and standard.

Union Steel Strikes

This management-labor relationship would work well for the next 30 years with both labor and management-owners keeping one another in check. Management would demand a "a day's work for a day's pay," and labor forced the owners to share in their profits. Their union-management relationship would creat a thriving econmey and highest standard of living for the middleclass in the history of the country. But in the 1980's, puppets to big business and the corporate machine, President Reagan and Vice-President Bush, ignored all Sherman Antitrust and United States Labor Laws. Since then, corporations and business have had free reign to bust unions by firering and replacing striking union workers whenever they see fit. Outsourcing of millions of middleclass jobs to third world nations offering slave labor for pennies an hour so that they can increse their profits not only cost the middleclass tens of millions of jobs, but billions in federal, state, county and city tax revenue. Businesses would rent an office out of the country to avoid paying taxes, and use their company's profits to buy up their competition to avoid showing a profit and paying taxes.

The 1980's and President Reagan & VP-George Bush Sr. time in office was discribed as the "me generation," or "the beginning of endless greed for one's self." Corporate and presidential policies since 1980's was not only the beginning of the end to labor unions, but to a thriving and expanding middleclass that fueler the United States economy for thirity years. Also in the 1980's brought deregulations to many corporate owned big businesses including the Savings & Loan Institutions that abused their freedoms from regulations that caused billions to be lost by its depositors with few employees being held accountable or prosecuted by the Justice Department. The lack of accounting regulations and tax cuts to the top 1% of wage earners also brought on corporate sinful greed by CEO's and their Directors costing investors hundreds of billions of dollars while most of the thieves either walked away with hundred-million dollar bonuses before being caught or after getting caught setttleing out of court with the U.S. Justice Department for pennies on a dollar in fines from what they stole and a few months in Federal "country-club" Prison. Some of the largest Corporations would be caught through to 2001 with very few serving time in jail.

By the mid-1990's the economy would be fueled by "the internet boom," with prosperity for many while manufacturing jobs continued to be lost to third world countries providing slave labor for pennies an hour. In 2000, for the first time in over a century, the United States showed a surplus of over $120 billion.

The United State of America can not be defeated militarily, but will economically from their own greed for individual material self-worth.
   - **Communist China President Mao Zedong**

From 2001-2006, the U.S. Justice Department as well as the Republican controlled U.S. Congress and White House ignored any type accountability or law regulations. In housing, banking regulations had been changed or ignored with no oversite, causing hundreds of thousands of mortgage foreclosures with banks and trust companies losing in the hundreds of billions of dollars as the home buyers lost their home. By 2008, there is little left to fuel the country's economy with a smaller middleclass, a $10 trillion national debt, a $9 trillion dollar trade deficit, a 40% falling value of the American Dollar, housing foreclosures in the billions lost, rising unemployed people, inflation on food from corporate greed and rising gasoline prices that tripled since 2001 while oil companies reported record profits. Big business and corporations had gotten what they wanted, no regulations as it was in the 1920s. Just like in the 1920s, corporations got too greedy causing the middleclass to shrink to where few had enough to keep the economy going. In President Hoover's day, as is today in 2008, the government's answer to the country's economic problem was to throw money to corporations with tax breaks and substidies with little effect on improving the economy instead of getting the unemployed back to work with tariffs that would protect the worker from cheap imports.

With every taxcut, the government must borrow more money, which caused the value of the American dollar to sink, which caused the price of imports, especially oil, to increase. Then when the price of imports increase and the cost of gasoline goes up, it caused delivery of all products to also increase. Inflation increased and in a short time, as was the case in the 1920s when Republicans also controlled all three branches of government, a depression hit. In 1927, 25% of all the country's wealth was at the top 1%...the same as it is in 2008.

But as it was in the 1920's, today some will benefit quite hansomly. Once again, JPMorgan Chase would use their ownership into the Federal Reserve to secure a low interest loan of $29 billion to buy Bear Stearns for pennies on the dollar; an acqusistion that is forcasted to make JPMorgan Chase over one billion dollars in the next year from Bear Stearns assets alone. The price tag of Bear Stearns first was reported at around $276 million, or $2.00 a stock share for a company who's stock only one year ago was at $176 a share. Grumblings within Wall Street has force JPMorgan to increase their offer, but no dought, will be well below its worth and give the buyers future profits in the tens of billions.

In 1980, America was the greatest manufacturing & creditor nation in the history of the world. After 28 years of pro-corporate Republican policies, in 2008 America is the most indebted & largest importer in the history of the world. In 1980, the top 1% wage earners made 8% of all wages made in the United States. By 2006, the top 1% wage earners made 20% of all wages made...a difference of 12% of all wages went from the poor & middleclass to the top 1% of the wealthy in 26 years of Reagan-Bush "trickle down economics" and Republican pro-corporate, pro-wealthy policies.

Chapter VIII
Beginning of Big Messes, the Eisenhower-Nixon Follies

President Eisenhower,(left) signs Interstate Highway System Bill as close friend & golfing buddy Senator Prescott Bush sits next to him. Senator Presctt Bush,(right) ready's his pawn, and newcomer to politics Dick Nixon for his first campaign.

Dwight D. Eisenhower took office on January 20th of 1953 and served two terms with Richard Nixon as vice-president. As President, he oversaw the end of the Korean War,(and didn't get assassinated), kept up the pressure on the Soviet Union during the Cold War, made nuclear weapons a higher defense priority, launched the Space Race and began the Interstate Highway System. He continued all the major New Deal programs still in operation, Social Security he expanded its programs and rolled them into a new cabinet-level agency, the Department of Health, Education and Welfare, while extending benefits to an additional ten million workers.

President Eisenhower,(above left) listens to Senator Prescott Bush, President Eisenhower(middle) shares laughs with President-elect John F. Kennedy and, Eisenhower (right) speaks with George Bush Sr., Prescott Bush's son.

Senator Prescott Bush during the years Eisenhower was President, was the most connect politician to not only the White House but to industry and the capitalists. His father, Samuel Bush, had worked for Frank Rockefeller, then replaced him upon Rockefeller's retirement as CEO at Buckeye Steel and was on the Board of Directors and major stockholder of the Federal Reserve in Cleveland, Ohio. Prescott Bush before serving as senator from 1952 to January of 1963, was a Wall Street executive banker and founding partner with Brown Brothers Harriman, where he met finacial partner to the firm and his future father in-law George Herbert Walker. Prescott with fellow "Skull & Bones" member, E. Rowland Harriman, and brother of Brown Brothers Harriman founder, W. Averall Harriman, set up Union Bank of New York to attend to German industrialist and Nazi finacial backer Fritz Thyseen's needs of laudering German money for gold, silver, American currency, fuel, steel and arms. He also help found and was on the board of directors to CBS. Prescott and his family's ties with the Rockefeller family continued to this day.

"Everything the Bush Family has, we owe thanks to the Rockefellers." - George W. Bush Sr., 2004

Senator Prescott Bush
& George W. Bush Sr.

Senators said President Eisenhower and vice-president Dick Nixon never made a move until consulting with Prescott Bush. According to Nixon's biogaphy, his personal and political ties with the Bush Family go back to 1946. Nixon claims he read a Los Angeles newspaper ad by the Orange County Republican Party and a wealthy group of businessmen headed by Prescott Bush, the father of George Bush Sr. They wanted a young candidate to run for Congress. Nixon applied and won the job to become a mouthpiece for the Bush group, progressing to the United States Senate and in 1952 to the vice-presidency.

Eisenhower was very knowledgable at first of the powers that had, and still controled politician Dick Nixon, as well as the capitalists/globalists that influenced and in some cases, controled the Prescott Bush Group. But during his first term as President, he fore saw the dangerous road the country would be directed down by the capitaliats influencing Prescott Bush who had always had control over Richard Nixon. With Nixon being a incumbet two term vice-president, he surely would become the next Republican canidate for president, and probably the next president of the United States; a position Eisenhower feared for the country.

President Eisenhower in 1956 asked Vice-President Nixon to step down from running with him for a second term. Nixon ignored Eisenhower's request and used his contact with Senator Prescott Bush to use his powerful influence within the Republican Party to secure Nixon's spot on the ticket.

Eisenhower-Nixon's Mistakes Toward Castro Costly

Fidel Castro arrived in the United States on April 15th, 1959 for a tour that was first planned to last until April 20th, but by American popular demand, extended to the 26th. Castro only four years early in 1955, with the blessing of the United State State Department visited for seven weeks Miami, New York and New Jersey to solicit funds for his revolution in Cuba.

In 1959, Castro's visit was one as a conquoring hero of the revolution he led and newly appointed Prime Minister by Cuba's President Manuel Urrutia Lleo. His public appearances at all hours of the day or night in Washington D.C. between April 15th to 20th, was to say he wasn't flirting with making Cuba a communist country. He also explained his agricultural proposal to give back the country's land to its people from the large foreign businesses that had abussively taken over and controled much of Cuba's farm land. Foreign ownership of land would be forbidden with farms being held to a maxium of 993 acres per owner, which would force the spread of farming prosparity to a muiltitude of Cubian citizens; rather than American and other foreign companies that monopolized the industry by unfairly destroying their smaller, individual, Cuban owned competition.

Castro confirmed his intention to steer the Revolution toward a moderate course with domecratic principles. On the 19th of April, after being driven to the Lincoln Memorial, he carifully read the Gettysburg Address and turned to the nearby crowd of people watching him and shouted. "This supported the ideal of the Cubain Revolution!" Later that day, and after being interviewed on "Meet the Press" television program, Castro visited the White House where he was snubbed by President Eisenhower. For some reason Eisenhower went golfing with Senator Prescott Bush instead. Castro had to settle with speaking to a powerless Vice-President Nixon.

Snubbing the Prime Minister of nearby Cuba was a mistake the United States would have to live with for decades to come. But one must ask, why would President Eisenhower snub Castro? Granted, Eisenhower would later be known as a "do nothing" President, and surely he was known as a "yes man" to the Republican Party and the powers behind it, including Prescott Bush, capitalist banks, industrialists and oilmen who finacially backed him in his only two campaigns for the only political office he held. They were the same backers Eisenhower would make them millions for with contracts to build the Interstate Highway System. He also protected his big business backers with his Eisenhower Doctrine that protected Western business interests in the Mideast, oil companies included. But the question remains, why would Eisenhower snub a conquoring hero to the Cuban people as well as thousands of Americans for ousting the brutal Cuban President as Batista, while speaking of freedom and democarcy for his people? Unless…those same capitalists that had promoted past wars for their own industrial and banking empirc's profits told him to do so through his close friend and golfing buddy, Senator Prescott Bush. Was the reason for the snubbing in hopes of a future war for profit with Cuba, or just a message to Castro of future retaliation against Cuba if he were to follow through of his proposals of giving back to the Cubian people their farming, industry and oil businesses? Such laws Castro was proposing would cost some of the most powerful capitalists in the United States millions of dollars of investments and future profits in Cuba.

Castro continued his tour including a well publicized speech at Princston University, meeting friends in Houston, Texas and a brief stop in Canada before returning to Cuba.

Although Castro's speeches continued to be "democracy with freedom for Cuban people" in natue, his distain towards the capitalist's "imperial business conquest in foreign countries" attitude never left him. The well educated Castro was once a respected lawyer in Havanna before taking up arms against the previous brutal and currupt Batista Government. He had seen how American companies had all but invaded and taken over Cuban businesses without care of how they harmed the enviornment or the Cuban people.

"I will lead Cuba's economic and cultural progress without sacrificing their freedoms." Castro would say. "I have no plans to nationalize land while the government legally exporpriate idle and unproductive land."

"Democarecy is the most beautiful political and social ideas." Castro would say many times. "Expecting and will allow, minority parties to develop even if it opposes his government."

Hearing such things repeatedly from Castro, one would have to say the United States couldn't ask for anything more…except to those American capitalists that had investments and/or had eyes for future profits in Cuba. Castro's "spread the Cuban wealth to the Cubans" would cost the capitalists millions and something had to be done to prevent it.

Castro was aware of how American corporations with the help of the CIA exploreted foreign country's resources and manipulated their government, which made him suspicous of the United State Government's intentions whenever dealing with them. In 1954, the democratically elected Guatemalan government of Colonel Jacobo Arbenz Guzmán was toppled by a group of Guatemalan army officers who invaded from Honduras and assisted covertly by the U.S. Central Intelligence Agency with Allen Dulles the Director. Before that, the directors of UFCO had lobbied to convince the Truman and Eisenhower administrations that Colonel Arbenz intended to align Guatemala with the Soviet bloc. Besides the disputed issue of Arbenz's allegiance to Communism, the directors of UFCO may have feared Arbenz's stated intention of purchasing uncultivated land from foreign companies (at the value declared in tax returns) and redistributing it among Native American peasants. The American Secretary of State John Foster Dulles was an avowed opponent of Communism whose law firm had represented United Fruit. His brother Allen Dulles was the director of the CIA. The brother of the Assistant Secretary of State for InterAmerican Affairs John Moors Cabot had once been president of United Fruit.

Dean Acheson
April 11th, 1893 - October 12th, 1971
Secretary of State 1949-1953
Advisor to Presidents: Roosevelt, Truman,
Eisenhower, Kennedy, Johnson & Nixon.

Dean Acheson attended Groton School and Yale College (1912–15), where he joined Scroll and Key Society and Harvard Law School from 1915 to 1918. Acheson was an American stateman, lawyer and played a central role in defining Untied States policy during the Cold War. He took part in creating many important institutions including the International Monetary Fund, World Bank, NATO and the early organizations that would become the European Union and World Trade Organization.

He designed the American/British/Dutch oil embargo that cut off 95 percent of Japanese oil supplies and escalated the crisis with Japan in 1941. Historians debate whether Roosevelt fully understood and approved the scope of the embargo, but there is no doubt Acheson knew it would produce war.

In 1944, Acheson played a central role in the Bretton Woods Conference as the head delegate from the State Department. At this conference the post-war international economic structure was designed. The conference was the birthplace of the International Monetary Fund, the World Bank, and the General Agreement on Tariffs and Trade, the last of which would evolve into the World Trade Organization.

His most famous decisions was convincing the nation to enter the Korean War in June of 1951 and was instrumental forming the U.S. policy toward Vietnam, persuading Truman to dispatch aid and advisors to French forces in Indochina.

As undersecretary to the United States Department of State during the Truman Presidency, Acheson is given credit for devising American policy and writing the "Truman Doctrine," that gave economic and military aid to Turkey and Greece to prevent them from falling to Communist Soviet Union. Believing the best way to contain Stalin's Communism and prevent future conflicts in Western Europe, he composed the "Marshell Plan" that gave economic assistance to European countries in need.

During the Cuban Missile Crisis, President John F. Kennedy called upon Acheson from retirement for advice, bringing him into the executive committee (ExComm), a strategic advisory group. Acheson wanted to invade Cuba with the full force of the United States Military, but was dispatched by Kennedy to France to brief de Gaulle and gain his support for the United States blockade of Cuba.

Acheson claimed to had a private conversation at length with Fidel Castro through an interpretor on April 20th of 1959. He expressed being very impressed with Castro, but forsaw him becoming a future problem to United States interests. Only two years later, Acheson said he couldn't remember ever speaking with Castro.

In 1960, Vice-President Nixon traveled the world seeking the presidency with Senator Prescott Bush's support every step of the way. Congressman Gerald Ford from Michigan and Prescott's son and owner of Zapata Petroleum Company, George Bush Sr., also helped Dick Nixon through out his political career to raise money.

During his second term as Vice-President, Nixon ordered CIA Director Allen Dulles to organize groups of anti-Castro Cubans and "soldiers of fortune" to first assassinate Fidel Castro, then take over Cuba. The CIA sponsored Operation 40 was a select group of assassins from the much larger Operation Zapata group that would invade Cuba. CIA agents labeled the invasion of Cuba "Operation Zapata," after the George Bush own off-shore oil drilling company because the Operation used their oil rig platform to spy of Cubian activity and their boats to transport the anti-Casto Cubans for the operation.

Operation 40

Vice-President George H.W. Bush Sr. sitting with friend Felix Rodriguez. Lt. and CIA Agent Rodriguez,(middle) and Lt. Luis Posada Carriles,(far right) were members of Operation 40 group of assassins aimed at Castro, then later used in the Kennedy Assassination.

Apart from Felix Rodriguez, other members were now infamous CIA agents and anti-Castro terrorists like Luis Posada Carriles, Orlando Bosch, Guillermo and Ignacio Novo Sampoll and later Watergate plumbers Frank Sturgis, Eugenio Martinez, Virgilio Gonzalez and E. Howard Hunt. Most of the Operation 40 members were recruited from JM/Wave, or Operation Zapsta, a much larger clandestine operation to train a Cuban exile army for the Bay of Pigs invasion. JM/Wave was headed by CIA official Theodore Shackley. James Files, the confessed gunman on the grassy knoll in the JFK Assassination, was recruited for the CIA by David Atlee Phillips on a recommendation of Ted Shackley. Shackley became CIA Director George Bush's deputy director for Covert Operations in 1976.

Hunt & Sturgis

Two person's name that kept popping up during several future investigations would be *E. Howard Hunt* and *Frank Sturgis*. They were members of the CIA's Operation 40 to kill Fidel Castro and invade Cuba, accused as being two of the "three tramps, arrested and released by Dallas Police shortly after President Kennedy was assassinated, and arrested during the Watergate burglary schandal. **E. Howard Hunt** joined the CIA in 1949 and became Mexico City's station chief in 1950, and supervised **William F. Buckley**. Little has been published regarding Buckley's work with the CIA, but in a 2001 a letter to author W. Thomas Smith, Jr., Buckley wrote:

"I did training in Washington as a secret agent and was sent to Mexico City. There I served under the direct supervision of Howard Hunt, about whom of course a great deal is known."

In a Nov. 1, 2005, editorial for the National Review, William F. Buckley recounted that:
When in 1951 I was inducted into the CIA as a deep cover agent, the procedures for disguising my affiliation and my work were unsmilingly comprehensive. It was three months before I was formally permitted to inform my wife what the real reason was for going to Mexico City to live. If, a year later, I had been apprehended, dosed with sodium pentothal, and forced to give out the names of everyone I knew in the CIA, I could have come up with exactly one name, that of my immediate boss (E. Howard Hunt, as it happened). In the passage of time one can indulge in idle talk on spook life. In 1980 I found myself seated next to the former president of Mexico at a ski-area restaurant. What, he asked amiably, had I done when I lived in Mexico? "I tried to undermine your regime, Mr. President." He thought this amusing, and that is all that it was, under the aspect of the heavens.

E. Howard Hunt helped devise Operation PBSUCCESS, the covert plan to overthrow Jacobo Arbenz, the elected president of Guatemala. Following assignments in Japan and Uruguay, Hunt was assigned to forge Cuban exile leaders in the United States into a broadly representative government-in-exile that would, after the Bay of Pigs Invasion, form a provisional government to take over Cuba. The failure of the invasion damaged his career.

Hunt told the Senate Watergate Committee in 1973 that he served as the first Chief of Covert Action for the CIA's Domestic Operations Division. He told the New York Times in 1974 that he spent about four years working for the division, beginning shortly after it was set up, in 1962, over the "strenuous opposition" of Richard Helms and Thomas H. Karamessines. **He said that the division was assembled shortly after the Bay of Pigs operation, and that "many men connected with that failure were shunted into the new domestic unit." He said that some of his projects from 1962 to 1966, which dealt largely with the subsidizing and manipulation of news and publishing organizations, "did seem to violate the intent of the agency's charter."**

Hunt was undeniably bitter about what he saw as President John F. Kennedy's lack of spine in overturning the Castro regime. In his autobiography, Give Us this Day, he wrote: *"The Kennedy administration yielded Castro all the excuse he needed to gain a tighter grip on the island of Jose Marti, then moved shamefacedly into the shadows and hoped the Cuban issue would simply melt away."*

Two pictures of E. Howard Hunt and one in the middle of the so-called "tramp."

The following year, 1971, Hunt was hired by Charles Colson, chief counsel to President Richard Nixon, and joined the President's Special Investigations Unit (alias White House Plumbers). Hunt's first assignment for the White House was a covert operation to break into the Los Angeles office of Daniel Ellsberg's psychiatrist, Dr. Lewis J. Fielding. In July 1971, Fielding had refused an FBI request for psychiatric data on Ellsberg. Hunt and Liddy cased the building in late August. The burglary, on September 3, 1971, was not detected, but no Ellsberg files were found. Also in the summer of 1971, Colson authorized Hunt to travel to New England to seek potentially scandalous information on Senator Edward Kennedy. Hunt sought and used CIA disguises and other equipment for the project.

Hunt's White House duties included assassinations and related disinformation. In September 1971, Hunt forged and offered to a Life magazine reporter top-secret State Department cables designed to prove that President Kennedy had personally and specifically ordered the assassination of Ngo Dinh Diem and his brother Ngo Dinh Nhu. Hunt told the Senate Watergate Committee in 1973 that he had fabricated the cables to show a link between President Kennedy and the assassination of Diem, a Catholic as was Kennedy, was to estrange Catholic voters from the Democratic party.

According to Seymour Hersh, writing in the The New Yorker, Nixon White House tapes show that after presidential candidate George Wallace was shot on May 15, 1972, Nixon and Colson agreed to send Hunt to the Milwaukee home of the gunman, Arthur Bremer, to place McGovern presidential campaign material there. The intention was to link Bremer with the Democrats. Hersh writes that, in a taped conversation:

"Nixon is energized and excited by what seems to be the ultimate political dirty trick: the FBI and the Milwaukee police will be convinced, and will tell the world, that the attempted assassination of Wallace had its roots in left-wing Democratic politics."

Hunt organized the bugging of the Democratic National Committee at the Watergate office building. A few days after the break-in, Nixon was recorded saying, to H. R. Haldeman:

(Note: From other tape recordings and interviews with people within the Nixon Administration and others that knew him well, Nixon would use a "code word" whenever speaking about the JFK Assassination. Nixon had always been a pawn to International Finacial Banker and Senator, Prescott Bush...and a indirect pawn to the people at the top responsible for ordering, carrying out and covering up the Assassination of President John F. Kennedy. President Nixon knew the penalty for crossing these powerful people, or challenging their power as President Kennedy did. At the time of the following recording, Nixon was President, the powerful people had gotten away with not only assassinating President Kennedy, but covering up their part in it. Nixon would never take the chance of making the deadly mistake of exposing these powerful group of people responsible for Kennedy's death, or ever take the risk of exposing anyone connected to it. So Nixon could deny any association with the assassination, or conversation pertaining to it, he used code words whenever he spoke about the JFK Assassination, which were *"Bay of Pigs thing."* As you read the following tape recorded conversation by the then President Nixon, know the *"Bay of Pigs thing"* within Nixon's works ment the "JFK Assassination.")

"Very bad, to have this fellow Hunt, ah, you know, ah, it's, he, he knows too damn much and he was involved, we happen to know that. And that it gets out that the whole, this is all involved in the Cuban thing, that it's a fiasco, and it's going to make the FBI, ah CIA look bad, it's going to make Hunt look bad, and it's likely to blow the whole, uh, "Bay of Pigs thing" which we think would be very unfortunate for CIA and for the country at this time, and for American foreign policy, and he just better tough it and lay it on them."

Hunt and fellow operative G. Gordon Liddy, along with the five arrested at the Watergate, were indicted on federal charges three months later. Hunt's wife, Dorothy, was killed in the December 8, 1972 plane crash of United Airlines Flight 553 in Chicago was a **message to him to keep his mouth shut on the** *"Bay of Pigs thing."* Congress, the Federal Bureau of Investigation (FBI), and the National Transportation Safety Board (NTSB) investigated the crash, found it to be an accident. Over $10,000 in cash was found in Dorothy Hunt's handbag in the wreckage. E. Howard Hunt eventually spent 33 months in prison on a conspiracy charge, and said he was bitter that he was sent to jail while Nixon was allowed to resign.

Give Us This Day, Hunt's book on the Bay of Pigs Invasion, was published late in 1973. In the book's foreword, he commented on the assassination of President John F. Kennedy as follows:

"Once again it became fashionable to hold the city of Dallas collectively responsible for his murder. Still, and let this not be forgotten, Lee Harvey Oswald was a partisan of Fidel Castro, and an admitted Marxist who made desperate efforts to join the Red Revolution in Havana. In the end, he was an activist for the Fair Play for Cuba Committee. But for Castro and the Bay of Pigs disaster there would have been no such "Committee." And perhaps no assassin named Lee Harvey Oswald."

On November 3, 1978, Hunt gave a security-classified deposition for the House Select Committee on Assassinations. The Assassination Records Review Board (ARRB) released the deposition in February 1996. Two newspaper articles published a few months before the deposition stated that a 1966 CIA memo linking Hunt to the assassination of President Kennedy had recently been provided to the HSCA. The first article, by Victor Marchetti—author of the book The CIA and the Cult of Intelligence (1974)—appeared in the Liberty Lobby newspaper The Spotlight on August 14, 1978. According to Marchetti, the memo said in essence, ***"Some day we will have to explain Hunt's presence in Dallas on November 22, 1963."*** Marchetti also wrote that Hunt, Frank Sturgis, and Gerry Patrick Hemming would soon be implicated in a conspiracy to kill John F. Kennedy.

The second article, by Joe Trento and Jacquie Powers, appeared in the Wilmington, Delaware Sunday News Journal six days later. It alleged that the purported memo was initialed by Richard Helms and James Angleton and showed that, shortly after Helms and Angleton were elevated to their highest positions in the CIA, they discussed the fact that Hunt had been in Dallas on the day of the assassination and that his presence there had to be kept secret. However, nobody has been able to produce this supposed memo, and the **1975 United States President's Commission on CIA activities within the United States, headed by Vice-President Nelson Rockefeller** determined that Hunt had been in Washington, DC on the day of the Assassination.

JFK Assassination allegations by a Hunt Family member

The April 5, 2007 issue of Rolling Stone contained an extensive article on Hunt, based in large part on an interview with his eldest son, Howard (nicknamed Saint John by his mother). It describes Hunt's alleged deathbed confessions of his supposed knowledge and indirect complicity in the JFK assassination. Among other things, the article claims that Hunt, in hand-written notes and a voice recording to Saint John, implicated Lyndon B. Johnson and CIA operative Cord Meyer as the key players in the JFK assassination conspiracy. According to Hunt's son, Hunt claimed the other assassin was a French gunman on the grassy knoll, often identified in other assassination theories as Lucien Sarti. Among the materials provided by Hunt to his son are several handwritten documents detailing the participants and chronology of events involved with the assassination plot, including a Chain of Command indicating the involvement of several CIA agents and placing then Vice-President Lyndon B. Johnson as head of their command.

On the April 28, 2007 edition of Coast to Coast Live hosted by Ian Punnett, a portion of an audio tape sent by Saint John Hunt containing his father's January 2004 recounting of activities of several of fellow operatives played on-air for the first time. In the tape, Hunt named Cord Meyer, Frank Sturgis, David Sánchez Morales, and David Atlee Phillips as participants in the assassination with Vice-President Lyndon Johnson apparently approving the assassination.

The following is a transcript of Hunt's testament on the audio tape clip:

I heard from Frank that LBJ had designated Cord Meyer, Jr. to undertake a larger organization while keeping it totally secret. Cord Meyer himself was a rather favored member of the Eastern aristocracy. He was a graduate of Yale University and had joined the Marine Corps during the war and lost an eye in the Pacific fighting. I think that LBJ settled on Meyer as an opportunist—paren.—(like himself)—paren.—and a man who had very little left to him in life ever since JFK had taken Cord's wife as one of his mistresses. I would suggest that Cord Meyer welcomed the approach from LBJ, who was after all only the Vice President at that time and of course could not number Cord Meyer among JFK's admirers— quite the contrary. As for Dave Phillips, I knew him pretty well at one time. He worked for me during the Guatemala project. He had made himself useful to the agency in Santiago, Chile where he was an American businessman. In any case, his actions, whatever they were, came to the attention of the Santiago station chief and when his resume became known to people in the Western hemisphere division he was brought in to work on Guatemalan operations. Sturgis and Morales and people of that ilk stayed in apartment houses during preparations for the big event. Their addresses were very subject to change, so that where a fellow like Morales had been one day, you'd not necessarily associated [sic] with that address the following day. In short, it was a very mobile experience. Let me point out at this point, that if I had wanted to fictionalize what went on in Miami and elsewhere during the run up for the big event, I would have done so. But I don't want any unreality to tinge this particular story, or the information, I should say. I was a benchwarmer on it and I had a reputation for honesty. I think it's essential to refocus on what this information that I've been providing you — and you alone, by the way — consists of. What is important in the story is that we've backtracked the chain of command up through Cord Meyer and laying [sic] the doings at the doorstep of LBJ. He, in my opinion, had an almost maniacal urge to become President. He regarded JFK, as he was in fact, an obstacle to achieving that. He could have waited for JFK to finish out his term and then undoubtedly a second term. So that would have put LBJ at the head of a long list of people who were waiting for some change in the executive branch.

Cord Meyer Jr. Mary Pinchot Meyer and Mary fatally shot in 1964

Cord Meyer Jr. an advocate for "one world government" and one of the founders of United World Federalists, spent 26 years of his life as a CIA Agent. Cord was a mid-level player in the JFK Assassination and cleanup man to it's coverup. In 1963 his x-wife, Mary Pinchot Meyer, was having an affair with President Kennedy and let it be known to close friends, she was keeping a diary. After her still unsolved murder in 1964, her diary was recovered, affair exposed and since destroyed by a close friend. Cord Meyer Jr. shortly before is impending death, blamed the same ones responsible for JFK murder to Mary's.

CIA's Operation Zapata

During 1959-60, CIA Director Allen Dulles and the Eisenhower administration, under the direction of Vice-President Nixon, began to assemble in south Florida the infrastructure for covert action against Cuba. This was the JM/WAVE capability, later formally constituted as the CIA Miami station. JM/WAVE was an operational center for the Eisenhower regime's project of staging an invasion of Cuba using a secret army of anti-Castro Cuban exiles, organized, armed, trained, transported, and directed by the CIA. The Cubans, called Brigade 2506, were trained in secret camps in Guatemala. According to reliable sources and published accounts, the CIA code name for the Bay of Pigs invasion was Operation Zapata, and the plan was so referred to by Richard Bissell of the CIA, one of the plan's promoters, in a briefing to President Kennedy in the Cabinet Room on March 29, 1961.

Ted Shackley   **David Sanchez Morales**

Ted Shackley's second man in command of JM/Wave and David Sanchez Morales, who is also working close with David Atlee Phillips, developed a reputation as "best CIA assassin for Latin America". Cuban State security officials speculate that Morales was the "dark complexed man" as seen by several witnesses in the 6th floor window of the Texas School Book Depository. Just after telling friends he was afraid of his "own people", and just before he was scheduled to testify for the House Select Committee of Assassinations, Morales died in 1977 of a sudden heart attack under mysterious circumstances. Under influence of alcohol, he had hinted to close friends that he had been involved in the Kennedy assassination (We took care of that bastard, didn't we?"). Morales was a big muscular man of very dark complexion, nicknamed "el Indio". Several witnesses on Dealey Plaza, most of whom were not called to testify before the Warren Commission, described a man fitting Morales. These witnesses saw such a man in the windows of the sixth floor of the Texas School Book depository shortly before Kennedy's motorcade passed by, as well as minutes after the shooting, fleeing from the back of the building with two other men in a station wagon resembling the one the Paine Family owned, whom Maria Oswald at the time was living with. A week after the JFK Assassination, in a letter from FBI Director J. Edgar Hoover and not released to the public for three decades after the JFK Assassination, George W. Bush Sr. is exposed to being a CIA Agent and reliable source of information to the FBI pertaining to the Cubans in Florida.

By mid-1960, all was in place for the capitalists with their pawn, Vice-President Nixon, leading in the polls to become the next President and sights on reclaiming their business interests in Cuba. **Operation Zapata** was ready for an invasion into Cuba once Dick Nixon took office. Unlike President Kennedy would later not do, a President Nixon would follow orders to have the United States Air Force provide air cover for the invading anti-Castro Cubians and soldiers of fortune, being trained in South America and southern Florida.

 The New York Times.

KENNEDY'S VICTORY WON BY CLOSE MARGIN;
HE PROMISES FIGHT FOR WORLD FREEDOM;
EISENHOWER OFFERS 'ORDERLY TRANSITION'

Controversities

Some Republicans and historians have alleged that Kennedy benefited from voter fraud, especially in Texas and Illinois, and that Nixon actually won the national popular vote despite the fact that Republicans tried and failed to overturn the results in both these states at the time--as well as in nine other states. These two states are important because if Nixon had carried both, he would have won the election in the electoral college. Kennedy won Illinois by a bare 9,000 votes, even though Nixon carried 92 of the state's 101 counties. Kennedy's victory in Illinois came from the city of Chicago, where Mayor Richard J. Daley held back much of Chicago's vote until the late morning hours of November 9. The efforts of Daley and the powerful Chicago Democratic organization gave Kennedy an extraordinary Cook County victory margin of 450,000 votes --- more than 10% of Chicago's 1960 population of 3.55 million --- thus (barely) overcoming the heavy Republican vote in the rest of Illinois. In Texas, some Republicans argued that the formidable political machine of Lyndon B. Johnson had stolen enough votes in counties along the Mexican border to give Kennedy the victory there. According to Nixon partisans, the Republican party urged Nixon to pursue recounts and challenge the validity of some votes for Kennedy, especially in the pivotal states of Illinois, Missouri and New Jersey, where large majorities in Catholic precincts handed Kennedy the election. Nixon publicly refused to call for a recount, saying it would cause a constitutional crisis; he also convinced Mazo and the Herald Tribune to not print any stories suggesting that the election had been stolen by the Democrats. Privately, however, Nixon encouraged

Republican National Chairman Thruston Morton to push for a recount, which Morton did in 11 states, keeping challenges in the courts into the summer of 1961; the only result was the loss of the State of Hawaii to Kennedy on a recount petitioned by the Kennedy campaign. Kennedy's defenders, such as historian Arthur M. Schlesinger, Jr., have argued that Kennedy's margin in Texas (46,000 votes) was simply too large for vote fraud to have been a decisive factor; in Illinois Schlesinger and others have pointed out that even if Nixon carried Illinois, the state alone would not have given him the victory, as Kennedy would still have won 276 electoral votes to Nixon's 246 (with 269 needed to win).

"We face a hostile ideology global in scope, atheistic in character, ruthless in purpose and insidious in method..." said President Eisenhower during his final speech in as President, then warned about what he saw as unjustified government spending proposals and continued with a warning that *"we must guard against the acquisition of unwarranted influence, whether sought or unsought, by the military-industrial complex... Only an alert and knowledgeable citizenry can compel the proper meshing of the huge industrial and military machinery of defense with our peaceful methods and goals, so that security and liberty may prosper together."*

President Eisenhower was worried about the direction some of the most powerful industrialists and bankers were attempting to take the country.

"There are a group of well financed and powerful Texians with influencial friends throughout the country and within our government power structure that wish to change America's way of living as we know it today and will do anything to accomplish their goals." **– President Eisenhower to his brother Feb. of 1961**

Chapter IX
Two Powerful Political Families of the 20th Century

Bush Family Empire

| Samuel | Prescott | George Sr. | George Jr. |

Samuel Prescott Bush, (October 4th, 1863 – February 8th, 1948), is son of Harriet Fay and Rev. James Smith Bush. Samuel grew up mostly in Columbus, Ohio and graduated in 1884 from Stevens Institute of Technology at Hoboken, New Jersey.

Bush took an apprenticeship with "Pittsburgh, Cinncinnati, Chicago and St. Louis Railroad Company" in Logansport, Indiana. He would first transfer to Dennison, Ohio, then to Columbus, Ohio where during 1891 became a Master Mechanic and in 1894 Superintendent of Motor Power.

Samuel married Flor Sheldon in 1894 and they had five children; one of which was Prescott.

In 1899, Bush moved to Milwaukee, Wisconson to work for Chicago, Milwaukee and St. Paul Railroad Company as Superintendent of Motive Power.

In 1901, he returned to Columbus, Ohio to work as General Manager for Buckeye Steel Casting Company that manufactured railway parts at the time and would later expand to small arms parts during World War I. The Company was run by Frank Rockefeller, brother of oil magnate John D. Rockefeller, and among their clients were railroads controlled by E.H. Harriman. (The Bush and Harriman Families would share a close business and personal relationship for decades to come.)

In 1908, Samuel replaced the retiring Frank Rockefeller at Buckeye Steel Casting Company as President, a position he would hold until 1927, and became one of the top industrialists of his generation. To the Company's employees, he was known as a ruthless manager that force the Company's managers to threaten employees with firing to get them to work the amount of days and hours he seem fit for higher profits. Profits and expanion was all that mattered to Bush and there were times when employees were forced to work twelve hour days, seven days a week. Replacing employees with the unemployed was common for all those complaining about work conditions, pay or hours they were forced to work.

Buckeye Steel Castings 1917

In 1918, Bush was appointed as Chief of Ordance, Small Arms and Ammunitions Section for the United States; giving him the authority to determine which American companies would supply United States and their allies fighting in World War I with small arms and ammunition. Samuel P. Bush during World War I was to the Rockefellers, what President G.W. Bush Jr. and Vice-President Dick Cheney are today to Halliburton, Dresser Company and other corporations receiving billions in no bid contracts with little accountability. (At one time, Prescott Bush ran Dresser Industries and his son, George W. Bush Sr., was a director and both held, and still hold stock in the company. In 1998, Halliburton bought Dresser Industries.) Percy Rockefeller ran Remmington Arms and Samuel Bush not only provided the Rockefellers with inside information to which companies were to receive contracts, as well as, directing over 65% of small arms and ammunition business from United States and their allies during World War I to Remmington Arms and Buckeye Steel Casting Company.

Samuel served on the **Board of Directors** and became a **major stockholder of the Federal Reserve Bank of Cleveland,** and the Hunnington National Bank of Columbus.

On February 8th, 1948 at the age of 84, Samuel Prescott Bush died in Columbus, Ohio.

**Buckeye Steel Castings
Samuel Prescott Bush - President**

Buckeye Steel Casting Company

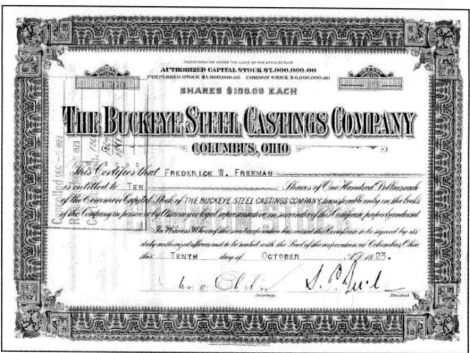

Buckeye Steel Casting Company

Samuel Bush's Family Home

Kennedy Family Beginning

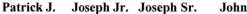

Patrick J.   Joseph Jr. Joseph Sr.   John   Robert,(Bobby), Ted, John

Patrick J. Kennedy, (January 14th, 1858 – May 18th, 1929), was the youngest of five children born to Patrick Kennedy, a poor Irish Roman Catholic immigrant to the United States, and Bridget Murphy. The couple's first son, John, died of cholera in infancy. Months after P.J.'s birth, his father also died of cholera. As the only man in the household, Patrick had to quit school at age 14 to work on the shipping docks of Boston's Eastside where he, his mother and three older sisters grewup. "P.J." as he was called, would later attend Boston College on a scholarship.

During the 1880s, Patrick began a business career by buying a saloon in Haymarket Square, Boston. In time he would buy a second saloon on the docks, then a third establishment in an upscale hotel named the Maverick House.

Before Kennedy was thirity, his prosparity allowed him to buy a whiskey importing business he named P.J. Kennedy and Company. His importing business made Patrick a leading figure in the Boston liquor trade.

Patrick J. Kennedy was known as very likable and always ready to help the less fortunate with a little cash and sensible advice.

Once Kennedy established himself in the business community, he devoted much of his time to public service. After serving five one-year terms in the Massachusetts House of Representatives, PK was elected to three two-year terms in the state senate. In 1888, as one of Boston's Democratic leaders, Patrick Kennedy gave a speech for Grover Cleveland at the National Convention in St. Louis. He also served on the Massachusetts State Election Commission, local fire commission and member of the Democratic "unofficial" Stradegy Board.

By the time of Patrick J. Kennedy's death in May of 1949, he also had investments in a coal company and a substancial amount of stock in Columbia Trust Company.

Prescott Sheldon Bush Family

Senator Prescott Bush and His Family—Three Generations

Prescott Sheldon Bush, (May 15th, 1895 – October 8th, 1972), was born in Columbus, Ohio to Flora (Sheldon) and Samuel Prescott Bush. His family's wealth and influence allowed Prescott Bush to attend only prevate schools of Douglas School in Columbus, Ohio, St. George's School in Newport, Rhode Island, New York, and in1913 enrolled at Yale University. Prescott would begin four consecutive generations of Bush family members to graduate from Yale and a member of one of the college's fraternity, Skull and Bones Secret Society.

After graduation, Bush served as a field artillery captain with the American Expeditionary Forces (1917-1919) during World War I. He received intelligence training at Verdun, France, and was briefly assigned to a staff of French officers.

In 1919, Prescott Bush went to work for the Simmons Hardware Company in St. Louis, Missouri.

On August 6th, 1921, Prescott married Dorthy Walker in Kennebunkport, Maine. They had five children, Prescott "Pressy" Bush Jr. born in 1922, George Herman Walker Bush in 1924 who was named after his grandfather, George Herbert Walker, Nancy in 1926, Jonathan in 1931 and William "Bucky" Bush in 1938.

108

In 1923, the Bush Family moved to Columbus, Ohio, where Prescott Bush went to work for the Hupp Products Company, where his business efforts generally failed and left in November 1923 to become president of sales for Stedman Products in South Braintree, Massachusetts.

In 1924, Bush was made a vice-president of Harriman & Company by his father-in-law, George Herbert Walker. Also employed by the company were E. Roland Harriman and Knight Woolley, Bush's Yale classmates and fellow Skull and Bones Secret Society members.

In 1925, Prescott moved his family to Greenwich, Connecticut to work for the United States Rubber Company of New York City as manager of the foreign division.

In 1931, Bush became a founding partner of Brown Brothers Harriman & Co. that was created through the 1931 merger of Brown Brothers & Company, a merchant bank founded in Philadelphia, Pennsylvania in 1818, and Harriman Brothers & Company, established in New York City in 1927 as A. Harriman & Company.

In the 1930's, under the oversight, direction and finacial backing of Brown Brothers Harriman & Company, Prescott's father-in-law, George Herbert Walker, and German industrialist, bank owner and Hitler's finacial backer to build the Nazi war machine, Fritz Thyseen, Union Bank Corporation of New York was set up by Prescott Bush, follow Skull & Bones Secret Society fraternity brother E. Rowland Harriman and Cornelis Lievense. With George Herbert Walker as the bank's president and Prescott Bush its Managing Director, Union Bank laundered millions of dollars of Fritz Thyseen profits into steel, coal, gold, silver, arms, American currency and bonds.

From 1944 to 1956, Bush was a member of the Yale Corporation, the principal governing body of Yale University and Board of Director of CBS TV.

In 1942, Prescott, a Republican conservative, got involved with the American Birth Control League and served as treasurer of the first campain of Planned Parenthood in 1947.

From 1947 to 1950, Bush served as Connecticut Republican finance chairman.

In 1950, Prescott was the Republican candidate for the United States Senate, but lost to William Benton by only 1,000 votes.

In 1952, Bush was elected to the United States Senate and served until January of 1963. During that time he became a close personel friend and golfing buddie with future President, Dwight Eisenhower.

Prescott Bush through the years became a staunch opponate of the Kennedy Family, especially President Kennedy's view for America and Kennedy's maternal grandfather, John "Honey Fitz" Fitzgerald.

On October 8th, 1972, Prescott Sheldon Bush Sr. died at the age of 77.

The Dutch Connection
By Attorney John Loftus
©. 2000-2002 John Loftus
7-2-2

John Loftus, is a former U.S. Department of Justice Nazi War Crimes prosecutor, the President of the Florida Holocaust Museum and the highly respected author of numerous books on the CIA-Nazi connection including The Belarus Secret and The Secret War Against the Jews, both of which have extensive material on the Bush-Rockefeller-Nazi connection.

John D. Rockefeller Sr. & Jr., Fitz Thyssen & Adolph Hitler, Prescott S. Bush.

For the Bush family, it is a lingering nightmare. For their Nazi clients, the Dutch connection was the mother of all money laundering schemes. From 1945 until 1949, one of the lengthiest and, it now appears, most futile interrogations of a Nazi war crimes suspect began in the American Zone of Occupied Germany. Multibillionaire steel magnate Fritz Thyssen-the man whose steel combine was the cold heart of the Nazi war machine-talked and talked and talked to a joint US-UK interrogation team. For four long years, successive teams of inquisitors tried to break Thyssen's simple claim to possess neither foreign bank accounts nor interests in foreign corporations, no assets that might lead to the missing billions in assets of the Third Reich. The inquisitors failed utterly.

Why? Because what the wily Thyssen deposed was, in a sense, true. What the Allied investigators never understood was that they were not asking Thyssen the right question. Thyssen did not need any foreign bank accounts because his family secretly owned an entire chain of banks. He did not have to transfer his Nazi assets at the end of World War II, all he had to do was transfer the ownership documents - stocks, bonds, deeds and trusts--from his bank in Berlin through his bank in Holland to his American friends in

New York City: Prescott Bush and Herbert Walker. Thyssen's partners in crime were the father and father-in-law of a future President of the United States.

The allied investigators underestimated Thyssen's reach, his connections, his motives, and his means. The web of financial entities Thyssen helped create in the 1920's remained a mystery for the rest of the twentieth century, an almost perfectly hidden underground sewer pipeline for moving dirty money, money that bankrolled the post-war fortunes not only of the Thyssen industrial empire...but the Bush family as well. It was a secret Fritz Thyssen would take to his grave.

It was a secret that would lead former US intelligence agent William Gowen, now pushing 80, to the very doorstep of the Dutch royal family. The Gowens are no strangers to controversy or nobility. His father was one of President Roosevelt's diplomatic emissaries to Pope Pius XII, leading a futile attempt to persuade the Vatican to denounce Hitler's treatment of Jews. It was his son, William Gowen, who served in Rome after World War II as a Nazi hunter and investigator with the U.S. Army Counter Intelligence Corps. It was Agent Gowen who first discovered the secret Vatican Ratline for smuggling Nazis in 1949. It was also the same William Gowen who began to uncover the secret Dutch pipeline for smuggling Nazi money in 1999.

A half-century earlier, Fritz Thyssen was telling the allied investigators that he had no interest in foreign companies, that Hitler had turned on him and seized most of his property. His remaining assets were mostly in the Russian Occupied Zone of Germany (which he knew were a write-off anyway). His distant (and disliked) relatives in neutral nations like Holland were the actual owners of a substantial percentage of the remaining German industrial base. As innocent victims of the Third Reich, they were lobbying the allied occupation governments in Germany, demanding restitution of the property that had been seized from them by the Nazis. Under the rules of the Allied occupation of Germany, all property owned by citizens of a neutral nation which had been seized by the Nazis had to be returned to the neutral citizens upon proper presentation of documents showing proof of ownership. Suddenly, all sorts of neutral parties, particularly in Holland, were claiming ownership of various pieces of the Thyssen empire. In his cell, Fritz Thyssen just smiled and waited to be released from prison while members of the Dutch royal family and the Dutch intelligence service reassembled his pre-war holdings for him.

Walker   Harriman   P. Bush   Allen Dulles   Fitz Thyssen   Hitler

The British and American interrogators may have gravely underestimated Thyssen but they nonetheless knew they were being lied to. Their suspicions focused on one Dutch Bank in particular, the Bank voor Handel en Scheepvaart, in Rotterdam. This bank did a lot of business with the Thyssens over the years. In 1923, as a favor to him, the Rotterdam bank loaned the money to build the very first Nazi party headquarters in Munich. But somehow the allied investigations kept going nowhere, the intelligence leads all seemed to dry up.

If the investigators realized that the US intelligence chief in postwar Germany, Allen Dulles, was also the Rotterdam bank's lawyer, they might have asked some very interesting questions. They did not know that Thyssen was Dulles' client as well. Nor did they ever realize that it was Allen Dulles's other client, Baron Kurt Von Schroeder who was the Nazi trustee for the Thyssen companies which now claimed to be owned by the Dutch. The Rotterdam Bank was at the heart of Dulles' cloaking scheme, and he guarded its secrets jealously.

Several decades after the war, investigative reporter Paul Manning, Edward R. Murrow's colleague, stumbled across the Thyssen interrogations in the US National Archives. Manning intended to write a book about Nazi money laundering. Manning's manuscript was a dagger at Allen Dulles' throat: his book specifically mentioned the Bank voor Handel en Scheepvaart by name, albeit in passing. Dulles volunteered to help the unsuspecting Manning with his manuscript, and sent him on a wild goose chase, searching for Martin Bormann in South America.

Without knowing that he had been deliberately sidetracked, Manning wrote a forward to his book personally thanking Allen Dulles for his "assurance that I was "on the right track, and should keep going.'"Dulles sent Manning and his manuscript off into the swamps of obscurity. The same "search for Martin Bormann"scam was also used to successfully discredit Ladislas Farago, another American journalist probing too far into the laundering of Nazi money. American investigators had to be sent anywhere but Holland.

And so the Dutch connection remained unexplored until 1994 when I published the book "The Secret War Against the Jews."As a matter of historical curiosity, I mentioned that Fritz Thyssen (and indirectly, the Nazi Party) had obtained their early financing from Brown Brothers Harriman, and its affiliate, the Union Banking Corporation. Union Bank, in turn, was the Bush family's holding company for a number of other entities, including the "Holland American Trading Company." It was a matter of public record that the Bush holdings were seized by the US government after the Nazis overran Holland. In 1951, the Bush's reclaimed Union Bank from the US Alien Property Custodian, along with their "neutral" Dutch assets. I did not realize it, but I had stumbled across a very large piece of the missing Dutch connection. Bush's ownership of the Holland-American investment company was the missing link to Manning's earlier research in the Thyssen investigative files. In 1981, Manning had written:

"Thyssen's first step in a long dance of tax and currency frauds began [in the late 1930's] when he disposed of his shares in the Dutch Hollandische-Amerikanische Investment Corporation to be credited to the Bank voor Handel en Scheepvaart, N.V., Rotterdam, the bank founded in 1916 by August Thyssen Senior." In this one obscure paragraph, in a little known book, Manning had unwittingly documented two intriguing points: 1) The Bush's Union Bank had apparently bought the same corporate stock that the Thyssens were selling as part of their Nazi money laundering, and 2) the Rotterdam Bank, far from being a neutral Dutch institution, was founded by Fritz Thyssen's father. In hindsight, Manning and I had uncovered different ends of the Dutch connection. After reading the excerpt in my book about the Bush's ownership of the Holland-American trading Company, retired US intelligence agent William Gowen began to put the pieces of the puzzle together. Mr. Gowen knew every corner of Europe from his days as a diplomat's son, an American intelligence agent, and a newspaperman. William Gowen deserves sole credit for uncovering the mystery of how the Nazi industrialists hid their money from the Allies at the end of World War II.

In 1999, Mr. Gowen traveled to Europe, at his own expense, to meet a former member of Dutch intelligence who had detailed inside information about the Rotterdam bank. The scrupulous Gowen took a written statement and then had his source read and correct it for error. Here, in summary form, is how the Nazis hid their money in America.

After World War I, August Thyssen had been badly burned by the loss of assets under the harsh terms of the Versailles treaty. He was determined that it would never happen again. One of his sons would join the Nazis; the other would be neutral. No matter who won the next war, the Thyssen family would survive with their industrial empire intact. Fritz Thyssen joined the Nazis in 1923; his younger brother married into Hungarian nobility and changed his name to Baron Thyssen-Bornemisza. The Baron later claimed Hungarian as well as Dutch citizenship. In public, he pretended to detest his Nazi brother, but in private they met at secret board meetings in Germany to coordinate their operations. If one brother were threatened with loss of property, he would transfer his holdings to the other.

To aid his sons in their shell game, August Thyssen had established three different banks during the 1920's -- The August Thyssen Bank in Berlin, the Bank voor Handel en Scheepvaart in Rotterdam, and the Union Banking Corporation in New York City. To protect their corporate holdings, all the brothers had to do was move the corporate paperwork from one bank to the other. This they did with some regularity. When Fritz Thyssen "sold" the Holland-American Trading Company for a tax loss, the Union Banking Corporation in New York bought the stock. Similarly, the Bush family invested the disguised Nazi profits in American steel and manufacturing corporations that became part of the secret Thyssen empire.

When the Nazis invaded Holland in May 1940, they investigated the Bank voor Handel en Scheepvaart in Rotterdam. Fritz Thyssen was suspected by Hitler's auditors of being a tax fraud and of illegally transferring his wealth outside the Third Reich. The Nazi auditors were right: Thyssen felt that Hitler's economic policies would dilute his wealth through ruinous war inflation. He had been smuggling his war profits out through Holland. But the Rotterdam vaults were empty of clues to where the money had gone. The Nazis did not know that all of the documents evidencing secret Thyssen ownership had been quietly shipped back to the August Thyssen Bank in Berlin, under the friendly supervision of Baron Kurt Von Schroeder. Thyssen spent the rest of the war under VIP house arrest. He had fooled Hitler, hidden his immense profits, and now it was time to fool the Americans with same shell game.

As soon as Berlin fell to the allies, it was time to ship the documents back to Rotterdam so that the "neutral" bank could claim ownership under the friendly supervision of Allen Dulles, who, as the OSS intelligence chief in 1945 Berlin, was well placed to handle any troublesome investigations. Unfortunately, the August Thyssen Bank had been bombed during the war, and the documents were buried in the underground vaults beneath the rubble. Worse, the vaults lay in the Soviet Zone of Berlin.

According to Gowen's source, Prince Bernhard commanded a unit of Dutch intelligence, which dug up the incriminating corporate papers in 1945 and brought them back to the "neutral" bank in Rotterdam. The pretext was that the Nazis had stolen the crown jewels of his wife, Princess Juliana, and the Russians gave the Dutch permission to dig up the vault and retrieve them. Operation Juliana was a Dutch fraud on the Allies who searched high and low for the missing pieces of the Thyssen fortune.

In 1945, the former Dutch manager of the Rotterdam bank resumed control only to discover that he was sitting on a huge pile of hidden Nazi assets. In 1947, the manager threatened to inform Dutch authorities, and was immediately fired by the Thyssens. The somewhat naive bank manager then fled to New York City where he intended to talk to Union Bank director Prescott Bush. As Gowen's Dutch source recalled, the manager intended "to reveal [to Prescott Bush] the truth about Baron Heinrich and the Rotterdam Bank, [in order that] some or all of the Thyssen interests in the Thyssen Group might be seized and confiscated as German enemy property. "The manager's body was found in New York two weeks later. Similarly, in 1996 a Dutch journalist Eddy Roever went to London to interview the Baron, who was neighbors with Margaret Thatcher. Roever's body was discovered two days later. Perhaps, Gowen remarked dryly, it was only a coincidence that both healthy men had died of heart attacks immediately after trying to uncover the truth about the Thyssens.

Neither Gowen nor his Dutch source knew about the corroborating evidence in the Alien Property Custodian archives or in the OMGUS archives. Together, the two separate sets of US files overlap each other and directly corroborate Gowen's source. The first set of archives confirms absolutely that the Union Banking Corporation in New York was owned by the Rotterdam Bank. The second set (quoted by Manning) confirms that the Rotterdam Bank in turn was owned by the Thyssens.

It is not surprising that these two American agencies never shared their Thyssen files. As the noted historian Burton Hersh documented: "The Alien Property Custodian, Leo Crowley, was on the payroll of the New York J. Henry Schroeder Bank where Foster and Allen Dulles both sat as board members. Foster arranged an appointment for himself as special legal counsel for the Alien Property Custodian while simultaneously representing [German] interests against the custodian."

No wonder Allen Dulles had sent Paul Manning on a wild goose chase to South America. He was very close to uncovering the fact that the Bush's bank in New York City was secretly owned by the Nazis, before during and after WWII. Once Thyssen ownership of the Union Banking Corporation is proven, it makes out a prima facie case of treason against the Dulles and Bush families for giving aid and comfort to the enemy in time of war.

PART TWO

The first key fact to be proven in any criminal case is that the Thyssen family secretly owned the Bush's Bank. Apart from Gowen's source, and the twin American files, a third set of corroboration comes from the Thyssen family themselves. In 1979, the present Baron Thyssen-Bornemisza (Fritz Thyssen's nephew) prepared a written family history to be shared with his top management. A copy of this thirty-page tome entitled "The History of the Thyssen Family and Their Activities" was provided by Gowen's source. It contains the following Thyssen admissions:

"Thus, at the beginning of World War II the Bank voor Handel en Scheepvaart had become the holding of my father's companies - a Dutch firm whose only shareholder was a Hungarian citizen..Prior to 1929, it held the shares of the August Thyssen Bank, and also American subsidiaries and the Union Banking Corporation, New York. The shares of all the affiliates were, in 1945, with the August Thyssen Bank in the East Sector of Berlin, from where I was able to have them transferred into the West at the last moment"

"After the war the Dutch government ordered an investigation into the status of the holding company and, pending the result, appointed a Dutch former general manager of my father who turned against our family.. In that same year, 1947, I returned to Germany for the first time after the war, disguised as a Dutch driver in military uniform, to establish contact with our German directors"

"The situation of the Group gradually began to be resolved but it was not until 1955 that the German companies were freed from Allied control and subsequently disentangled. Fortunately, the companies in the group suffered little from dismantling. At last we were in a position to concentrate on purely economic problems -- the reconstruction and extension of the companies and the expansion of the organization."

"The banking department of the Bank voor Handel en Scheepvaart, which also functioned as the Group's holding company, merged in 1970 with Nederlandse Credietbank N.V. which increased its capital. The Group received 25 percent. Rockefeller's Chase Manhattan Bank holds 31%. The name Thyssen-Bornemisza Group was selected for the new holding company."

Thus the twin US Archives, Gowen's Dutch source, and the Thyssen family history all independently confirm that President Bush's father and grandfather served on the board of a bank that was secretly owned by the leading Nazi industrialists. The Bush connection to these American institutions is a matter of public record. What no one knew, until Gowen's brilliant research opened the door, was that the Thyssens were the secret employers of the Bush family.

But what did the Bush family know about their Nazi connection and when did they know it? As senior managers of Brown Brothers Harriman, they had to have known that their American clients, such as the Rockefellers, were investing heavily in German corporations, including Thyssen's giant Vereinigte Stahlwerke. As noted historian Christopher Simpson repeatedly documents, it is a matter of public record that Brown Brother's investments in Nazi Germany took place under the Bush family stewardship.

When war broke out was Prescott Bush stricken with a case of Waldheimers disease, a sudden amnesia about his Nazi past? Or did he really believe that our friendly Dutch allies owned the Union Banking Corporation and its parent bank in Rotterdam? It should be recalled that in January 1937, he hired Allen Dulles to "cloak" his accounts. But cloak from whom? Did he expect that happy little Holland was going to declare war on America? The cloaking operation only makes sense in anticipation of a possible war with Nazi Germany. If Union Bank was not the conduit for laundering the Rockefeller's Nazi investments back to America, then how could the Rockefeller-controlled Chase Manhattan Bank end up owning 31% of the Thyssen group after the war?

It should be noted that the Thyssen group (TBG) is now the largest industrial conglomerate in Germany, and with a net worth of more than $50 billion dollars, one of the wealthiest corporations in the world. TBG is so rich it even bought out the Krupp family, famous arms makers for Hitler, leaving the Thyssens as the undisputed champion survivors of the Third Reich. Where did the Thyssens get the start-up money to rebuild their empire with such speed after World War II?

The enormous sums of money deposited into the Union Bank prior to 1942 is the best evidence that Prescott Bush knowingly served as a money launderer for the Nazis. Remember that Union Banks' books and accounts were frozen by the U.S. Alien Property Custodian in 1942 and not released back to the Bush family until 1951. At that time, Union Bank shares representing hundreds of millions of dollars worth of industrial stocks and bonds were unblocked for distribution. Did the Bush family really believe that such enormous sums came from Dutch enterprises? One could sell tulip bulbs and wooden shoes for centuries and not achieve those sums. A fortune this size could only have come from the Thyssen profits made from rearming the Third Reich, and then hidden, first from the Nazi tax auditors, and then from the Allies.

The Bushes knew perfectly well that Brown Brothers was the American money channel into Nazi Germany, and that Union Bank was the secret pipeline to bring the Nazi money back to America from Holland. The Bushes had to have known how the secret money circuit worked because they were on the board of directors in both directions: Brown Brothers out, Union Bank in.

Moreover, the size of their compensation is commensurate with their risk as Nazi money launderers. In 1951, Prescott Bush and his father in law each received one share of Union Bank stock, worth $750,000 each. One and a half million dollars was a lot of money in 1951. But then, from the Thyssen point of view, buying the Bushes was the best bargain of the war.

The bottom line is harsh: It is bad enough that the Bush family helped raise the money for Thyssen to give Hitler his start in the 1920's, but giving aid and comfort to the enemy in time of war is treason. The Bush's bank helped the Thyssens make the Nazi steel that killed allied soldiers. As bad as financing the Nazi war machine may seem, aiding and abetting the Holocaust was worse. Thyssen's coal mines used Jewish slaves as if they were disposable chemicals. There are six million skeletons in the Thyssen family closet, and a myriad of criminal and historical questions to be answered about the Bush family's complicity. ___

First published September, 2000
This article is provided courtesy of Dr. Leonard G. Horowitz and Tetrahedron Publishing Group www.tetrahedron.org
http://www.tetrahedron.org/articles/new_world_order/bush_nazis.html

Brown Brothers Harriman & Company

W. Averall Harriman* Robert Lovett* George Herbert Walker* Prescott S. Bush*
Founders not pictured: E. Roland Harriman*, Knight Woolley*, Moreau Delano,
Thatcher Brown, Louis Curtis*, Granger Kent Costikyan* and Ray Morris*.
*Denotes members of SKULL & BONES SECRET SOCIETY

Brown Brothers Harriman today, is the oldest and largest privately own banking partnership in the United States and are the lone trustee for Skull & Bone's "Russell Trust Association." Founded in 1931, the firm was a silent partner in the "Business Plot" to overthrow President Roosevelt. They were the Wall Street connection for the Nazis. Four of their many subsidiary companies they controlled were seized by the United State Government under the "Trading with the enemy Act." Union Bank of New York was contrived and ran by Prescott Bush to do business with the German industrial empire of Fritz Thyssen, who financed Hitler and the Nazis. Although Prescott owned only 1 of 4,000 shares, he was given E. Roland Harriman's 3,991 voting shares to run the Bank as he saw fit. Union Bank laundered German money for the Nazis in exchange of U.S. Treasury Bonds, gold, steel, coal and arms.

W. Averall Harriman's main properties included: Brown Brothers, Harriman & Co; Union Pacific Railroad; Merchant Shipping Corporation; and various venture capital investments including the Polaroid Corporation. Harriman's associated properties included: the Southern Pacific Railroad (including the Central Pacific Railroad), Illinois Central Railroad; Wells Fargo & Co.; the Pacific Mail Steamship Co.; American Shipping & Commerce (HAPAG), the American Hawaiian Steamship Co., United American Lines Co.; the Guarantee Trust Company, Dresser Company and the Union Banking Corporation. In 1998 Halliburton merged with Dresser Industries, which included Kellogg. Prescott Bush was a director of Dresser Industries, which is now part of Halliburton. Former United States president George H. W. Bush worked for Dresser Industries in several positions from 1948–1951, before he founded Zapata Corporation. The Bush family members had holding in Brown Brothers, Harriman & Company, Union Bank Corporation and Dresser Industries. Dresser Industries, (along with M.W. Kellogg which it bought in 1988), merged with their biggest rival, Halliburton Company in 1998.

In 2001, Dresser Inc. after buying back their equity from Halliburton, is owned by a private equity firm name First Reserve Corporation, who's owners we can't find.

(Pictured from left to right.) Dorothy & Prescott Bush, Fitz Thyseen, Ford & Nixon, Eisenhower & Prescott, Nixon & Prescott.

The Bush & would-be assassin John Hinckly Connection

Vice president George H.W. Bush, father of the current president, George Bush, Jr., assumed the duties of the presidency briefly after the shooting and nearly became president as Reagan almost died from the shooting. A bullet missed his aorta by less than an inch.

The Bush and Hinckley families go back to the oil-wildcatting days of the 1960s in Texas. (Ironically, they go back even farther in a genealogical sense, since the have a common ancestor in Samuel Hinckley, who lived in the late 1600s.)

Jo Ann Moore Hinckley & John Sr.   **John Hinckley Jr.**

Bush for Reagan?

President Ronald Reagan   **Vice-President George W. Bush Sr.**

The relationship was much closer between George Bush, Sr., and John Hinckley, Sr., whose families were neighbors for years in Houston. John Hinckley, Sr., contributed to the political campaigns of Bush, Sr., all the way back to Bush's running for Congress, and he supported Bush against Reagan for the 1980 Republican presidential nomination. Bush, Sr., and Hinckley, Sr., were both in the oil business. When the Hinckley oil company, Vanderbilt Oil, started to fail in the 1960s, Bush, Sr.'s, Zapata Oil financially bailed out Hinckley's company. Hinckley had been running an operation with six dead wells, but he began making several million dollars a year after the Bush bailout.

Scott Hinckley, John's brother, was scheduled to have dinner at the Denver home of Neil Bush, Bush, Sr.'s, son (and of course the current president's brother) the day after the shooting. At the time, Neil Bush was a Denver-based purchaser of mineral rights for Amoco (one of Rockefeller companies), and Scott Hinckley was the vice president of his father's Denver-based oil business.

On the day of the shooting, NBC news anchor John Chancellor, eyebrows raised, informed the viewers of the nightly news that the man who tried to kill the president was acquainted with the son of the man who would have become president had the attack succeeded. As a matter of fact, Chancellor reported in a bewildered tone, Scott Hinckley and Neil Bush had been scheduled to have dinner together at the home of the (then) vice-president's son (Neil) the very next night.

The story of the Bush-Hinckley connection was reported on the AP and UPI newswires and in some newspapers, including the Houston Post, which apparently originated the story. It was also reported in Newsweek magazine. Then the story about one of the strangest coincidences in presidential assassination history simply disappeared. (AP story is quoted in its entirety at the end of this article, not for commercial use but solely to be used for the educational purposes of research and open discussion.)

Scott Hinckley (above) and Neil Bush (above)

Neil at the time of the shooting was working for Rockefeller Family's Standard Oil Company, now known as ExxonMobil Oil. Neil is best known as a member of the board of directors of Denver-based Silverado Savings and Loan during the 1980s'. According to a piece in Salon, Silverado's collapse cost taxpayers $1 billion. Although Bush was not indicted on criminal charges, a civil action was brought against him and the other Silverado directors by the Federal Deposit Insurance Corporation; it was eventually settled out of court, with Bush paying $50,000 as part of the settlement, as reported in the Style section of the Washington Post. In July 1999, Bush made at least $798,000 on three stock trades in a single day of a company where he had been employed as a consultant. The company, Kopin Corporation of Taunton, Massachusetts, announced good news about a new Asian client that sent its stock value soaring. In 1999, Bush co-founded Ignite, a learning, educational software corporation. To fund Ignite, Bush raised $23 million from U.S. investors, including his parents, as well as businessmen from Taiwan, Japan, Kuwait, the British Virgin Islands and the United Arab Emirates, according to documents filed with the Securities and Exchange Commission. In 2002, Bush signed a consulting contract that paid $2 million dollars in stock over five years to work for Grace Semiconductor Manufacturing Corp., a firm backed by Jiang Mianheng, the son of former Chinese President Jiang Zemin, plus $10,000 for every board meeting he attends. Bush frequently travels to the Middle East, Europe and Asia to negotiate deals and raise capital for various businesses. According to court filings from his divorce, in 2000 he was paid $1.3 million for such work. This includes $642,500 as a commission for introducing an Asian investor to the owners of an American high-tech company. In Asia, Bush accompanied Sun Myung Moon on his world peace tour.

In reference to whether the current president, George W. Bush, knew the would-be assassin, John Hinckley, Bush said at the time, "It's certainly conceivable that I met him or might have been introduced to him. I don't recognize his face from the brief, kind of distorted thing they had on TV and the name doesn't ring any bells. I know he wasn't on our staff. I could check our volunteer rolls." There is no record that he ever did this or ever commented after further reflection and seeing better photographs.

Neil Bush used a similar line in denying he knew John Hinckley. "I have no idea," he said. "I don't recognize any pictures of him. I just wish I could see a better picture of him." Besides all of the family ties, Neil Bush lived in Lubbock, Texas, throughout much of 1978, where Reagan shooter Hinckley lived from 1974-1980. During this period, in 1978, Neil Bush served as campaign manager for the current president's unsuccessful run for Congress.

Neil's wife, Sharon Bush, who is writing an expose of the family, said, at the time, that Scott Hinckley was coming as a date of a girl friend of hers. "I don't even know the brother. From what I've heard, they are a very nice family and have given a lot of money to the Bush campaign. I understand he was just the renegade brother in the family." The dinner date was canceled.

Ironically, Scott Hinckley was called on the carpet by the U.S. Department of Energy on the day Reagan was shot. The DOE told Hinckley it might place a $2 million penalty on his company.

Marvin Pierce Bush

President G.W. Bush & Marvin   Marvin Bush   Marvin Bush

Marvin is son to former President George Walker Bush Sr. and younger brother to President George Walker Bush Jr. From 1993 until June 2000, he was on the board of directors of the Sterling, Virginia company Stratesec (formerly known as Securacom), which had contracts to provide security for United Airlines, Dulles International Airport, and the World Trade Center. The Securacom/Stratesec company was publicly traded and backed by an investment firm, the Kuwait-American Corporation. In 1996, Marvin Bush had 53,000 shares in the company's stock, which he bought at 52 cents a share. In 1997, the stock traded at $8.50 a share. Marvin P. Bush was a principal in a company. According to its present CEO, Barry McDaniel, the company had an ongoing contract to handle security at the World Trade Center "up to the day the buildings fell down." Stratesec (Securacom) differs from other security companies which separate the function of consultant from that of service provider. The company defines itself as a "single-source" provider of "end-to-end" security services, including everything from diagnosis of existing systems to hiring subcontractors to installing video and electronic equipment. It also provides armored vehicles and security guards.

The World Trade Center was destroyed just days after a heightened security alert was lifted at the landmark 110-story towers, security personnel said yesterday [September 11]. Daria Coard, 37, a guard at Tower One, said the security detail had been working 12-hour shifts for the past two weeks because of numerous phone threats. But on Thursday [September 6], bomb-sniffing dogs were abruptly removed. Pre-9/11 World Trade Center Power-Down. On the weekend of 9/8, 9/9 there was a 'power down' condition in WTC tower 2, the south tower. This power down condition meant there was no electrical supply for approx 36 hrs from floor 50 up... "Of course without power there were no security cameras, no security locks on doors and many, many 'engineers' coming in and out of the tower."

Marvin Bush is a former director of HCC Insurance Holdings, and is currently listed as an advisor to the board of directors. HCC, formerly Houston Casualty Company, is a publicly traded insurance company on the New York Stock Exchange. In a release on its official website dated September 13, 2007, HCC had what it called a "small participation in the World Trade Center property insurance coverage and some of the surrounding buildings".

Prescott Bush Jr.'s company was allowed to sell Communist China communication satellites even though there was an embargo against such sales. The fact his brother, George Bush Sr. was President at the time probably had something to do with it. Prescott Jr. had already built the first golf course in Communist China. Since George Bush Sr. was appointed by family close friend Dick Nixon as ambassador to Communist China, the Bush Family have had a close business relationship with China.

Joseph P. Kennedy Family

Joseph Patrick Kennedy, (September 6th, 1888 – November 18th, 1969) was born in Boston, Massachusetts, to Rose Fitzgerald and Patrick J. Kennedy. Joseph's home growing up was a prosperous and comfortable one, thanks to his his father's, Patrick, successful saloon business, investments, and an influential role in local politics.

Kennedy followed in the footsteps of several older cousins by attending Harvard College. At Harvard he focused on becoming a social leader, working energetically to gain admittance to the prestigious Hasty Pudding Club. While at Harvard he joined the Delta Upsilon fraternity and played on the baseball team.

In 1912, after graduating from Harvard, Joseph took his first job as a state employed bank examiner.

In 1913, Columbia Trust Bank, in which his father held significant amount of stock shares, was under threat from being taken over. Kennedy borrowed $45,000 from family and friends to buy back control and at age 25 and was rewarded by being elected the bank's president; making him the youngest bank president in America.

In 1914, Joe married Rose Fitzgerald, daughter of Boston's Democratic Mayor and the most recognized politician in the city, John "Honey Fitz" Fitzgerald. The had nine children, Joseph Jr. born in 1915, John in 1917, Rosemary in 1918, Kathleen in 1920, Eunice in 1921, Patrica in 1924, Robert in 1925, Jean in 1928 and Edward in 1932.

Kennedy emerged as a highly successful entrepreneur with an eye for value. He turned a handsome profit from ownership of Old Colony Realty Associates, Inc., which bought distressed real estate.

Although skeptical of American involvement in World War I, he sought to participate in war-time production as an assistant general-manager of Bethlehem Steel, a major shipyard in Quincy, Massachusetts. There he oversaw the production of transports and warships critical to the war. This job brought him into contact with the Assistant Secretary of the Navy, Franklin Delano Roosevelt.

In 1919, he joined the prominent stock brokerage firm of Hayden, Stone & Co. where he became an expert in dealing in the unregulated stock market of the day, engaging in tactics that would later be labeled insider trading and market manipulation; which Kennedy would make illegal after President Roosevelt appointed him Chairman of the United States Securities and Exchange Commission, (SEC).

In 1923 he set up his own investment company and became a multi-millionaire during the bull market of the 1920s and got out of the market in 1928, one year before it crashed.

In March of 1926, Kennedy moved to Hollywood to focus running a studio. He would make huge profits from reorganizing and refinancing several studios. In October of 1928, he formally merged his film companies FBO and KAO to form Radio-Keith-Orpheum (RKO) and made a large amount of money in the process. Then, keen to buy the Pantages Theatre chain, which had 63 profitable theaters, Kennedy made an offer of $8 million. It was declined. Joe then stopped distributing his movies to Pantages. Still, Alexander Pantages declined to sell. However, when Pantages was later charged and tried for rape, his reputation took a battering and he accepted Kennedy's revised offer of $3.5 million. It is estimated that Kennedy made over $5 million from his investments in Hollywood.

Kennedy was reputed to be an importer of alcoholic drinks from Canada into the USA during Prohibition, although allegations were never proven. After Prohibition ended, Kennedy consolidated an even larger fortune when his company, Somerset Importers, became the exclusive American agent for Gordon's Dry Gin and Dewar's Scotch. Anticipating the end of Prohibition, he assembled a large inventory of stock, which he later sold for a profit of millions of dollars when Prohibition was repealed in 1933.

Joe invested this money in residential and commercial real estate in New York, and Hialeah Race Track in Hialeah, Florida. His most important purchase was the largest office building in the country, Chicago's Merchandise Mart, which gave his family an important base in that city and an alliance with the Irish-American political leadership there.

In 1934, Kennedy was appointed Chairman of the United States Securities and Exchange Commission (SEC). He reforming work was widely praised, as investors realized the SEC was protecting their interests. One of the criticial reforms was the requirement of companies to regularly file financial statement with the SEC which were then made public for its stockholders. Up until 1934, financial reports were kept private except to such powerful investment houses as J.P. Morgan and elitist capitalists as the Rockefellers. This requirement broke what some saw as an information molopoly maintianed by only the few, and cost them millions in future profits.

In 1935, Joseph left the SEC to take over the Maritime Commission, which built on his wartime experience in running a major shipyard.

In the 1930s, Father Charles Coughlin became perhaps the most prominent Roman Catholic spokesman on political and financial issues with a radio audience that reached millions every week. Speaking from his parish, Royal Oak Shrine of the Little Flower in suburban Detroit, he was a strong supporter of Roosevelt in 1932. But Coughlin broke with the president in 1934 and became a bitter opponent in his weekly, anti-communist, anti-Federal Reserve and isolationist radio talks. Roosevelt sent Kennedy and other prominent Irish Catholics to praise and speak with Coughlin. But Coughlin swung his support to Huey Long in 1935 and then to a third party in 1936. Kennedy strongly supported the New Deal and believed as early as 1933 that Coughlin was "becoming a very dangerous proposition" as an opponent of Roosevelt and "an out and out demagogue." Kennedy worked with Roosevelt, Bishop Francis Spellman and Eugenio Cardinal Pacelli (later Pope Pius XII) who was supportive of the World Court in a successful effort to get the Vatican to shut the anti-World Court Coughlin down in 1936. Coughlin later returned to the air and in 1940 and Kennedy battled against his influence among the Irish regarding Coughlin's stance against self-interest imperialism.

Father Charles Coughlin, the Radio Priest from Shrine of the Little Flower in Royal Oak, Michigan

In 1938, Roosevelt appointed Kennedy as the United States Ambassador to the Court of St. James's (Britain). Kennedy's Irish and Catholic status did not bother the British; indeed he hugely enjoyed his leadership position in London society, which stood in stark contrast to his outsider status in Boston. Kennedy rejected the warnings of Winston Churchill that compromise with Nazi Germany was impossible; instead he supported Prime Minister Neville Chamberlain's policy of appeasement in order to stave off a second world war that would be a more horrible "armageddon" than the first. Shortly before the Nazi aerial bombing of British cities began in September 1940, Kennedy sought a personal meeting with Hitler, again without State Department approval, "to bring about a better understanding between the United States and Germany." Kennedy argued strongly against giving aid to Britain. "Democracy is finished in England. It may be here," stated Ambassador Kennedy, Boston Sunday Globe of November 10, 1940. In a one simple statement, Joe Kennedy ruined any future chances of becoming United States president, effectively committing political suicide. While Blitzkrieg bombs fell daily on England, Nazi troops occupied Poland, Belgium, the Netherlands, and France, Ambassador Kennedy unambiguously and repeatedly stated his belief that the war was not about saving democracy from National Socialism (Nazism) or Fascism. In the now-infamous, long, rambling interview with two newspaper journalists, Louis M. Lyons of the Boston Globe and Ralph Coglan of the St. Louis Post-Dispatch, Kennedy opined:

"It's all a question of what we do with the next six months. The whole reason for aiding England is to give us time." ... "As long as she is in there, we have time to prepare. It isn't that she's [Britain is] fighting for democracy. That's the bunk. She's fighting for self-preservation, just as we will if it comes to us." ... "I know more about the European situation than anybody else, and it's up to me to see that the country gets it,"

When the American public and Roosevelt Administration officials read his quotes on democracy being "finished", and his belief that the Battle of Britain wasn't about "fighting for democracy.", all of it being just "bunk", they realized that Ambassador Kennedy could not be trusted to represent the United States. In the face of national public outcry, he was offered the chance to fall on his sword, and he submitted his resignation later that month.

Joe Kennedy was a fiercely ambitious individual who thrived off competition and winning. And, in his eyes, the ultimate prize was being president of the United States. Joe Kennedy wanted his first son, Joseph Kennedy Jr. to become president, but after his death in WWII, he became determined to make his second oldest son, John F. Kennedy, president.

Joe Kennedy was consigned to the political shadows after his remarks during WWII that "Democracy is finished...", and he remained an intensely controversial figure among U.S. citizens because of his suspect business credentials, his Roman Catholicism, his opposition to Roosevelt's foreign policy, and his support for Joseph McCarthy. As a result, his presence in John F. Kennedy's presidential campaign had to be stymied. Having him in the spotlight would hurt John, making it look as if it were his father who was running for president. However, Joe Kennedy still drove the campaign behind the scenes. He played a central role in planning strategy, fundraising, and building coalitions and alliances. Joe supervised the spending and to some degree the overall campaign strategy, helped select advertising agencies, and was endlessly on the phone with local and state party leaders, newsmen, and business leaders. He had met thousands of powerful people in his career, and often called in his chips to help his sons. He would use this to his son's advantage.

On December 19, 1961, at the age of 73, Kennedy suffered a major stroke. He survived, but lost all power of speech, and was left paralyzed on his right side. As a result, he was confined to a wheelchair for the rest of his life. Despite being severely disabled from the stroke, Kennedy remained aware of the tragedies that befell his family until his own death, on November 18, 1969, two months after his eighty-first birthday.

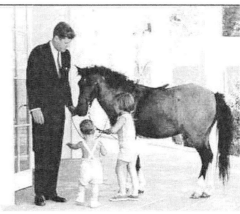

Chapter X
President John F. Kennedy & Wolves in Sheep's Clothing

Kennedy's presidency signified "out with the old, in with the new."

The pro-fascist capitalists that endure twelve years of Roosevelt after failing in the 1933 "Business Plot" had to be scratching their heads on how they let this happen to themselves and their plans of a "one world business."

President Kennedy's inaugural address on January 20th, 1961 had to make the fascist industrialists and bankers cringe.

"...my fellow citizens, we observe today not a victory of party, but a celebration of freedom symbolizing an end, as well as a beginning-signifying renewal as well as change...This world is different. ...We dare not forget today that we are the heir to the first revolution. Let the word go forth from this time and place, to friend and foe alike, that the torch has been passed to a new generation of Americans-born in this century, tempered by war, disciplined by a hard and bitter peace, proud of our ancient heritage...

President Kennedy's "New Frontier!"

President John F. Kennedy   **President Franklin D. Roosevelt**

Like President Roosevelt before him, President Kennedy symbolized a breath of fresh to American citizens, but represented everything the fascist corporatist didn't want in a president. Roosevelt's "New Deal" gave the out-of-work worker hope for a better future and retirerees a better quality of life with the addition of Social Security. Kennedy also believed in helping those who had little and desired a fair balance of "pay & profit" between worker and their employee.

President Roosevelt's policied reflected in his quotes.

"The test of our progress is not whether we add abundance to those that have much, but whether we provide to those who have too little."

"We cannot always build the future for our youth, but build our youth for our future."

"We must remember an oppression, any injustice, any hatred is a wedge designed to attack our civilization."

"...the only thing we have to fear, is fear itself."

With Kennedy in the White House, the capitalists from industry and banking institutions, who also were the major stockholders of the Federal Reserve, no longer had an ally to invade and retake their investments in Cuba. History had proved to them that members of the Kennedy Family could not be relied on to take their side against a common population, much less to invade a country for them. They believed Joseph P. Kennedy had turned on them during Franklin D. Roosevelt's Presidency when as chairman of the

Securities and Exchange Commission, he sided with the common investor and forced companies to make public their quarterly finacial reports. Up until then, only the powerful capitalists had privy to such vital information that allowed them a far greater upper hand in investments and manipulation of stocks on Wall Street. Kennedy had cost them millions in future profits by writing regulation for business and banking, and now Fidel Castro was also costing them millions.

Wolves in Sheep's Clothing!

FBI Director J. Edgar Hoover   **CIA Director Allen Dulles**

John Edgar Hoover (January 1, 1895 – May 2, 1972), was the Director of the Federal Bureau of Investigation (FBI) of the United States. He remained director for 48 years until his death. Hoover's leadership spanned eight presidential administrations, including the times of Prohibition, the Great Depression, World War II, the Korean War, the Cold

War, and the Vietnam War. Hoover exceeded and abused his authority, criticism that grew especially strong in the 1960s. He investigated individuals and groups because of their political beliefs rather than their suspected criminal activity, as well as using the FBI for other illegal activities, such as burglaries and illegal wiretaps. Hoover spied upon tens of thousands of suspected subversives and radicals, maintaining a list of 12,000 Americans suspected of disloyalty with the intention of detaining them and to do so by suspending the writ of habeas corpus.

In 1956, Hoover formalized a covert dirty tricks program under the name COINTELPRO. This program COINTELPRO was first used to disrupt the Communist Party, and later such organizations and individuals as the Black Panther Party, Martin Luther King, Jr., SCLC, the Ku Klux Klan and others indifferent to his way of thinking. Its methods included infiltration, burglaries, and illegal wiretaps, planting forged documents, spreading false rumors about key members of target organizations, inciting violence and arranging murders. In 1975, the activities of COINTELPRO were investigated by the Senate Church Committee and declared illegal and contrary to the Constitution.

Hoover amassed power by collecting files containing large amounts of compromising and potentially embarrassing information on many powerful people, especially politicians.

Jack Anderson   **Actress Jean Seberg**   **Rev. Martin Luther King Jr.**

In the 1950s, Hoover's unwillingness to focus FBI resources on the Mafia after Jack Anderson exposed the vast reach of the Mafia's organized crime network, led to Hoover's retaliation of harassment towards Anderson lasted into the 1970s. Hoover undermined the reputations of members of the civil rights movement including actress Jean Seberg and Martin Luther King, Jr.

Presidents Harry Truman and Lyndon B. Johnson considered firing Hoover but didn't because the political cost would of been too great. Richard Nixon twice called in Hoover with the intent of firing him, but changed his mind when meeting with Hoover. **Sources close to President John F. Kennedy have revealed the President spoke openly of replacing Hoover during his second term.**

Hoover personally directed the FBI investigation into the assassination of President John F. Kennedy. The House Select Committee on Assassinations issued a report in 1979 critical of the performance by the FBI, the Warren Commission as well as other agencies. The report also criticized what it characterized as the FBI's reluctance to thoroughly investigate the possibility of a conspiracy to assassinate the president. The HSCA further reported that Hoover's FBI "was deficient in its sharing of information with other agencies and departments." As a result, various conspiracy theories abound regarding the negligence of Hoover's leadership in performing due diligence with regard to the JFK assassination.

After several denials, investigative news reporters finally got Hoover to admit that he was in Dallas, Texas the night before and the day of, the Kennedy Assassination, but refused to say why he was there or details of what he did during that time.

In a letter from J. Edgar Hoover (next page), dated November 29th 1963 and only seven days after the JFK Assassination, Hoover identified George W. Bush Sr. as a CIA agent that had been a reliable source for information of the Miami-Cuban community.

Date: November 29, 1963

To: Director
          Bureau of Intelligence and Research
          Department of State

From: John Edgar Hoover, Director

Subject: ASSASSINATION OF PRESIDENT JOHN F. KENNEDY
          NOVEMBER 22, 1963

          Our Miami, Florida, Office on November 23, 1963, advised
that the Office of Coordinator of Cuban Affairs in Miami advised
that the Department of State feels some misguided anti-Castro
group might capitalize on the present situation and undertake an
unauthorized raid against Cuba, believing that the assassination
of President John F. Kennedy might herald a change in U. S. policy,
which is not true.

          Our sources and informants familiar with Cuban matters in
the Miami area advise that the general feeling in the anti-Castro
Cuban community is one of stunned disbelief and, even among those
who did not entirely agree with the President's policy concerning
Cuba, the feeling is that the President's death represents a great
loss not only to the U. S. but to all of Latin America. These
sources knew of no plans for unauthorized action against Cuba.

          An informant who has furnished reliable information in
the past and who is close to a small pro-Castro group in Miami
has advised that these individuals are afraid that the assassination
of the President may result in strong repressive measures being
taken against them and, although pro-Castro in their feelings,
regret the assassination.

          The substance of the foregoing information was orally
furnished to Mr. George Bush of the Central Intelligence Agency and
Captain William Edwards of the Defense Intelligence Agency on
November 23, 1963, by Mr. W. T. Forsyth of this Bureau.

1 - Director of Naval Intelligence

REC-38 62-109060—1396

Allen Welsh Dulles (April 7, 1893 – January 29, 1969) was the first civilian and the
longest serving (1953-1961) Director of the U.S. Central Intelligence Agency and a
member of the Warren Commission. Between stints of government service, Dulles was a
corporate lawyer and partner at Sullivan & Cromwell who worked closely with Brown
Brothers, Harriman and Companies.

From its earliest involvement in the formation of J. P. Morgan financed Edison General Electric Company in 1882 and J. P. Morgan's United States Steel Corporation in 1901, to its present work with leaders of the global economy in the 21st century, Sullivan & Cromwell has been closely involved in the affairs of some of America's and the world's greatest industrial, commercial and financial enterprises.

During and after World War II individual members of the firm, including partners such as John Foster Dulles and Arthur Dean, also played important roles in domestic politics and international affairs. The firm benefited from doing business with the Nazi regime, and throughout 1934, Dulles was a very public supporter of Hitler. In 1935, Dulles closed Sullivan & Cromwell's Berlin office; later he would cite the closing date as 1934, no doubt in an effort to clear his reputation by shortening his involvement with Nazi Germany.

John Foster Dulles' brother Allen Dulles also worked for Sullivan & Cromwell and was the key person that diverted investigators from looking into the "Industrialist and Nazi financial backer Fritz Thyssen German money laundering through the Dutch Bank Thyssen owned to Union Bank Corporation of New York that was owned by Thyssen and Brown Brothers, Harriman and Company." Union Bank Corp. was run by Director Prescott Bush who was given the voting power of E. Rowland Harriman's 3,991 shares of the Bank's total 4,000 shares so that Prescott could run the Bank as he seen fit to. Bush's father-in-law, George Herbert Walker, served as the Bank's President. Partner Robert MacCrate served as Counsel to New York Governor Nelson D. Rockefeller and as Special Counsel to the Department of the Army for its investigation of the My Lai Massacre.

Allen Dulles was born on April 7, 1893, in Watertown, New York, and grew up in a family where public service was valued and world affairs were a common topic of discussion. Dulles was the son of a Presbyterian minister, the younger brother of John Foster Dulles, Eisenhower's Secretary of State and Chairman and Senior Partner of Sullivan & Cromwell, and the grandson of John W. Foster, another U.S. Secretary of State and brother to diplomat Eleanor Lansing Dulles. His uncle (by marriage) Robert Lansing also was a U.S. Secretary of State. Dulles was appointed to become head of operations in New York for the Coordinator of Information (COI), taking over offices staffed by Britain's MI6 in Rockefeller Center. The COI was the precursor to the Office of Strategic Services, renamed in 1942.

During the 1930s Allen Dulles was transferred from Britain to Berne, Switzerland for the rest of World War II, and notably was heavily involved in the controversial and secret Operation Sunrise. Operation Sunrise was a series of secret negotiations conducted in March 1945 in Switzerland between representatives of the Nazi Germany and the U.S. to arrange a local surrender of German forces in northern Italy. Dulles became the station chief in Berne, Switzerland, for the newly formed Office of Strategic Services (the precursor to the CIA), a logical one.

Dulles' CIA Operation Paperclip assimilated Nazi scientists into the American establishment by obscuring their histories and short circuiting efforts to bring their true stories to light. Although the program officially ended in September 1947, those officers and others carried out a conspiracy until the mid-fifties that bypassed both law and presidential directive to keep Paperclip going. Neither Presidents Truman nor Eisenhower was informed that their instructions were ignored.

In 1953, Dulles became the first civilian Director of Central Intelligence. Under Dulles's direction, the CIA created MK-Ultra, a top secret mind control research project which was managed by Sidney Gottlieb. Dulles also personally oversaw Operation Mockingbird, a program which influenced American media companies as part of the "New Look."

At Dulles' request, President Eisenhower demanded that Senator McCarthy discontinue issuing subpoenas against the CIA. Documents made public in 2004 revealed that the CIA had broken into McCarthy's Senate office and intentionally fed disinformation to him in order to discredit him.

In 1957, the CIA picked up an important tool known as the U-2 Spy Plane.

Dulles established Operation 40; later known to CIA agents as Operation Zapata, a group presided over by Vice-President Richard Nixon. Their first operation against Cuba came on 4th March, 1960, La Coubre, a ship flying a Belgian flag, exploded in Havana Bay. It was loaded with arms and ammunition destined for the armed forces of the government of Fidel Castro. Operation 40 not only continued in sabotage operations against Cuba, but evolved into a team of assassins. One member, Frank Sturgis, claimed: *"this assassination group (Operation 40) would upon orders, naturally, assassinate either members of the military or the political parties of the foreign country that you were going to infiltrate, and if necessary some of your own members who were suspected of being foreign agents... We were concentrating strictly in Cuba at that particular time."*

Dulles went on to be successful with the CIA's first attempts at removing foreign leaders by covert means. Notably, the elected Prime Minister Mohammed Mossadegh of Iran was deposed in 1953 (via Operation Ajax), and President Arbenz of Guatemala was removed in 1954. The Guatemalan coup was called Operation PBSUCCESS. Dulles was on the Board of Director of the United Fruit Company. Dulles saw these kinds of clandestine activities as an essential part of the struggle against communism.

141

Dulles would also over see several assassination attempts on the life of Fidel Castro using an assortment of devices and plans, as well as different groups of organized organizations such as the Mafia, and individuals conspiring on their own to kill Castro. Surprising at the time, Dulles ironically not only served as a vital member of the Warren Commission, but seen fit not to let the Commission members know of the many failed CIA attempts on Castro's life. **(In 1966, the Warren Commission Report on the JFK Assassination would be first discredited after investigative reporter, Geraldo Rivera, on his ABC' show Good Morning America courageously and under pressure from ABC Inc. not to, showed to the public the "Zapruder Film" of the assassination of President John F. Kennedy. A following documentary on CBS, which Prescott Bush was co-founder of the station and on their Board of Directors, in 1967 was met with continued interference by Warren Commission member John McCloy, budget cuts impairing the documentary's authenticity of events of the Assassination, and omitted facts in CBS's hands that would of shed more light on the events of the Assassination as well as further discrediting the credibility of the Warren Commission Report.)**

Bay of Pigs, Invasion of Cuba

Cuba's Fidel Castro made it illegal for foreigners or foreign corporations to own property, thus throwing out of Cuba all American corporations and individuals with high priced investments, and costing them millions of dollars. In March of 1960, at the encouragement of Senator Prescott Bush and President Eisenhower approval, under the oversight of then Vice-President Nixon and the direction of CIA Director Allen Dulles, plans to assassination Fidel Castro and invade Cuba. Training camps for counter-revolutionary insurgents composed of anti-Castro Cubans and a wide range of international "soldiers of fortune and assassins" were set up in southern Florida and Guatemala. Along with Allen Dulles, other CIA agent's involvement in the Cuba invasion planning was directors Richard Bissell, Charles Cabell and agent George W. Bush Sr. along with other agents.

Accounts of what actually happen have varied over the years, and what is now known is that President Kennedy reluctantly went along with the planned invasion only if United States involvement be disguised sufficiently so the public wouldn't be aware of America's participation. CIA Director Dulles assured Kennedy that America's footprints wouldn't be on any facet of the operation, but in fact, few people within the Miami Cuban community didn't know of the planned invasion. So it's wasn't surprising that Fidel Castro was alerted before hand and was ready with 20,000 troops on April 17th, 1961 to combat and capture the 1,500 invading anti-Castro Cubans.

After the Allen Dulles led "Bay of Pigs" failed invasion turned into a total international embarassment for the United States, President Kennedy forced Dulles, CIA directors Richard Bissell and Charles Cabel to resign.

"I will splinter the CIA into a thousand pieces and scatter it into the winds."
- President John F. Kennedy

Fidel Castro's Dilemma

Only three years earlier in April of 1959, the leader of Cuba's revolution Fidel Castro had freely visited the United States and Vice-President Nixon at the White House. He was hailed by most as a conquering hero for defeating the brutal Presidency of Fulgencio Batista and was indirectly helped by the United States and the Allen Dulles directed CIA.

All possibility of allying himself with the United States fell apart when Castro returned Cuban land to his people from American corporations. Fidel decreed that no Cuban land could be owned by foreign individuals or corporations. A lawyer by trade before taking up arms and leading the revolution, Castro from past experience looked at American corporation's involvement into Cuban business as a cancer eating away at the soul of his country. It was obvious to Castro, that if he wished to have the United States as an ally, he also had to allow American corporations a free hand in doing business within Cuba, which Fidel wouldn't allow.

After the *Bay of Pigs Invasion,* did Castro have any choice but to turn to the Russians for protection? Knowing that the United States had trained anti-Castro Cubans and gave limited air support to them when invading, Fidel had to be wondering, what's next, a full invasion from the United States Military?

Cuba Missile Crisis

In another CIA involvement of Cuba and continued desire to take back control of American corporation's investments, on October 14th of 1962, a U-2 Spy Plane took photographs of missile silos under construction. President Kennedy again was faced with a dilemma; either confront Fidel Castro directly about having future missiles pointed at the United States only 90 miles away or be known for being soft on communism.

The "Joint Chiefs of Staff" unanimously agreed that only a full scaled missile attack followed by an invasion was the only solution. Others within his administration wanted an air assault on the missile sites. But Kennedy showed a calmer approach to the problem and ordered a quarantine of Cuba.

On October 22nd, Kennedy announced on TV that the U.S. Navy surrounded the island to inspect all boats headed for Cuba. Later, the public would find out that five destroyer battleships, two frigates and a submarine were used for the blockade. This not only inflamed Castro, but also Soviet Premier Nikita Khrushchev, who ordered a fleet of U.S.S.R. war ships toward Cuba for a head-to-head confrontation with the United States. For several hours, the United States and the U.S.S.R. were as close to war and nuclear exchange as they had or ever would be. American citizens stayed glued to the TV or radio for the latest news of a Soviet-American confrontation that could escalate into an all out nuclear war. By October 23rd, and until the morning of the 28th, Americans went to bed not knowing if nuclear exchanges began, they would never wake up again.

Both left and right picture's President Kennedy and Soviet Premier Nikita Khrushchev in 1961 months before the Cuban Missile Crisis. Middle picture is Kennedy meeting with Cabinet during Crisis.

On October 28th, the Kennedy-Khrushchev Pact was announced. Khrushchev would dismantle and remove Soviet missiles from Cuba while the United States promised not to invade Cuba in the future. Later the public would find out Kennedy would also agreed to remove American missiles pointed at the U.S.S.R. from Turkey, which were scheduled to be taken out the following summer which the U.S.S.R. didn't know about. Although the Joint Chiefs of Staff opposed the agreement Kennedy made with Khrushchev, they were force to abide by it. Some would accuse Kennedy as being soft on Communism. War hawk General LeMay told Kennedy *"it was the worst defeat in the country's history."* LeMay and others continued to encourage the President to invade Cuba, but Kennedy refused. Kennedy's calmness and decision not to invade probably saved the lives of tens of thousands of Americans, if not millions, since years later the United States would learn the entire extent of U.S.S.R.'s weapons in Cuba was far greater than what they thought Cuba had at the time.

Cuba and especially Fidel Castro would do fine without having the United States as their ally. History has shown Fidel Castro beat the United States at almost every level. The United States trade embargo had little effect on Castro or Cuba, since America was just about the only country in the world that continued the embargo. Presidents that followed Kennedy in need of the anti-Castro vote to win Florida have patronized those Cubans demanding revenge against Castro in the form of keeping a trade embargo against Cuba.

Sadly, these anti-Castro Cubans who lived well under the brutal Batista Administration, would rather keep an embargo against Castro than lift the embargo and be able to visit their family and friends in Cuba. Castro in 2008 announced his retirement, over 45 years after taking power.

Vietnam

In the early 1941, France and Japan were attempting to occupy different parts of Vietnam while Ho Chi Minh led a struggle for independence with support, clandestinely, by the United States Office of Strategic Services, (CIA). Minh would be jailed in China for months, then released in 1943 to return to Vietnam to continue his fight to make Vietnam an independent country from France. In 1945, Minh as Chairman of the Provisional Government (Premier of the Democratic Republic of Vietnam), petitioned American President Harry Truman for support for Vietnamese independence, but was rebuffed due to French pressure on the U.S. On September 2, 1945, after Emperor Bao Dai's abdication, Hồ Chí Minh read the Declaration of Independence of Vietnam, under the name of the Democratic Republic of Vietnam. With violence between rival Vietnamese factions and French forces spiraling, the British commander, General Sir Douglas Gracey declared martial law. On September 24, 1945, the Viet Minh leaders responded with a call for a general strike. Once America turned their back on their World War II ally, and Minh had no choice but to look to China for help against the French forces. In September of 1945, a force of 200,000 Chinese Nationalists arrived in Hanoi. Hồ Chí Minh made arrangements with their general, Lu Han, to dissolve the Communist Party and to hold an election which would yield a coalition government. When Chiang Kai-Shek later traded Chinese influence in Vietnam for French concessions in Shanghai, Hồ Chí Minh had no choice but to sign an agreement with France on March 6, 1946, in which Vietnam would be recognized as an autonomous state in the Indochinese Federation and the French Union. By this time, the United State was funding 87% of France's expenses in Vietnam. The agreement soon broke down, due in part France's insistence on occupying Vietnam and Minh wanting Vietnam to be independent. The purpose of the agreement was to drive out the Chinese army from North Vietnam. Fighting broke out against the French soon after the Chinese army left and Hồ Chí Minh was captured by a group of French soldiers led by Jean-Etienne Valluy at Việt Bắc, but was able to escape.

In 1950, Ho turned to U.S.S.R. and China to protect him and Vietnam from France, which all three countries decided it would be China's responsibility to assist Vietnam. The 1954 Geneva Accords required that a national election would be held in 1956 to reunite Vietnam under one government. However, the government of South Vietnam, now under the leadership of Ngo Dinh Diem, refused the proposed election and instead prepared for war. Following the Geneva Accords, there was to be a 300-day period in which people could freely move between the zones of the two Vietnams. Some 900,000 to 1 million Vietnamese, mostly Roman Catholic, left for South Vietnam, while a much smaller number, mostly communists, went from South to North. This was partly due to propaganda claims by a CIA mission led by Colonel Edward Lansdale that the Virgin

Mary had moved south out of distaste for life under Communism. Some Canadian observers claimed that some were forced by North Vietnamese authorities to remain against their will.

President Eisenhower would send to Vietnam "so called advisors" to assist South Vietnam in the fighting. In 1959, Hồ's government began to provide active support for the National Liberation Front in South Vietnam via the Ho Chi Minh Trail, which escalated the fighting that had begun in 1957.

In South East Asia, Kennedy followed Eisenhower's lead by using limited military action to fight the Communist forces ostensibly led by Ho Chi Minh. Proclaiming a fight against the spread of Communism, Kennedy enacted policies providing political, economic, and military support for the unstable French-installed South Vietnamese government, which included sending 16,000 military advisors and U.S. Special Forces to the area. Kennedy also agreed to the use of free-fire zones, napalm, defoliants and jet planes. U.S. involvement in the area continually escalated until regular U.S. forces were directly fighting the Vietnam War in the next administration. The Kennedy Administration increased military support, but the South Vietnamese military was unable to make headway against the pro-independence Viet-Minh and Viet Cong forces.

"I see the chickens have come to roost, my boy!" MacArthur said to President Kennedy. "You just happened to have moved into the chicken house."

"Anyone wanting to commit American ground troops on mainland Asia, should have his head examined." forewarned General MacArthur to President Kennedy.

By July 1963, Kennedy faced a crisis in Vietnam. The Administration's response was to assist in the coup d'état of the Catholic President of South Vietnam, Ngo Dinh Diem. In 1963, South Vietnamese generals overthrew the Diem government, arresting Diem and later killing him (though the exact circumstances of his death remain unclear). Kennedy sanctioned Diem's overthrow, but not his death. One reason for the support was a fear that Diem might negotiate a neutralist coalition government which included Communists, as had occurred in Laos in 1962.

Dean Rusk, Secretary of State

"This kind of neutralism...is tantamount to surrender."

It remains a point of controversy among historians whether or not Vietnam would have escalated to the point it did had Kennedy served out his full term and possibly been re-elected in 1964. Fueling this speculation are statements made by Kennedy and Johnson's Secretary of Defense Robert McNamara that Kennedy was strongly considering pulling out of Vietnam after the 1964 election. In the film "The Fog of War", not only does McNamara say this, but a tape recording of Lyndon Johnson confirms that Kennedy was planning to withdraw from Vietnam, a position Johnson states he disapproved of. Additional evidence is Kennedy's National Security Action Memorandum (NSAM) #263 on October 11, 1963 that gave the order for withdrawal of 1,000 military personnel by the end of 1963.

When President Kennedy looked at the problems the Office of Strategic Services and later the Allen Dulles led CIA got the United States into, it's a no wonder he wanted to destroy the Central Intelligence Agency. They had needlessly gotten the United States involved in Indonesia and backed the occupying force of France instead of Ho Chi Minh's desire for an independent Vietnam. Minh had asked the Truman Administration for help against French occupation and got turned down, forcing him to look for help from China and U.S.S.R...Just as Cuba's Fidel Castro would be forced to look for protection from a future invasion from the United States after the "Bay of Pigs" Allen Dulles led CIA invasion.

Iraq, land of Mobil, Bechtel and British Petroleum

In 1963, the CIA backed a coup against the government of Iraq headed by General Abdel Karim Kassem, who five years earlier had deposed the Western-allied Iraqi monarchy. The CIA helped the new Baath Party government led by Abdul Salam Arif in ridding the country of suspected leftists and Communists. In a Baathist bloodbath, the government used lists of suspected Communists and other leftists provided by the CIA, to systematically murder untold numbers of Iraq's educated elite. The victims included hundreds of doctors, teachers, technicians, lawyers and other professionals as well as military and political figures. The U.S. sent arms to the new regime, weapons later used against the same Kurdish insurgents the U.S. supported against Kassem and then abandoned. American and UK oil and other interests, including Mobil, Bechtel and British Petroleum, were conducting business in Iraq since the end of World War I.

President Kennedy no friend to big business

President Kennedy believed there should be a fair balance of power and profit sharing between ownership and labor. He backed President Roosevelt's "New Deal." In 1962 he pressured the steel industry into reversing price increases that Kennedy considered dangerously inflationary.

Kennedy's trade policies differed with the capitalists

A Reagan-Bush type NAFTA free trade agreement between United States and Canada covering all automobiles and their parts was proposed, but Kennedy refused to sign it. In doing so, he sighted that such an agreement is unfair to the United States and would cost thousands of Americans their jobs while startng the country on a trade path of no return.

Soon after President Kennedy's Assassination, President Johnson signed such a treaty.

President Kennedy signs the anti-business "Equal Pay Act" for women.

Chapter XI
Motive for Assassination

If history has taught us anything, it is that the United States is not run by our Presidents or Congressmen, but by those capitalists with industrial and financial empires that also are major stockholders of the United States Federal Reserve Central Banking System. The Federal Reserve Act of 1913 gave 12 private bankers endless worldwide power and changed America forever. Anyone attempting to take away such power became expendable by assassination or whatever means necessary.

"Who ever controls the volume of money in any country, is absolute master of all their industry and commerce."

- Paul Warburg, author of the Federal Reserve Act

"Before the passage of this Act, the New York bankers could only dominate the reserves of New York. Now we are able to dominate the bank reserves of the entire country."

- Senator Nelson W. Aldrich, Father in-law to John D. Rockefeller Jr.

"Give me the power to issue a nation's money and I care not who writes their laws."
- Amschel Rothschild, founder of the Rothschild Banking Empire

*"If the American people ever allow private banks to control the issue of their money, first by inflation, then by deflation, the banks and corporations that will growup around them,
will deprive the people of their property until their children wake up homeless on their continent their fathers conquered."* - Thomas Jefferson

Alfred Crozier, lawyer, author of 1912 book "U.S. Money vs Corporation Currency."

Testified for the Senate Committee, attacking the Aldrich-Vreeland Plan Act of 1908 as a tool of Wall Street and with a private own central bank system, the nation would no longer be free.

"When the President signs this bill, the invisible government of the monetary power will be legalized... The worst legislation crime of the ages is perpetrated by this banking and currency bill." - Charles A. Lindbergh Sr., 1913

"We shall have world government, whether or not we like it. The only question is whether world government will be achieved by conquest or consent." Paul Warburg author of Federal Reserve Act

"...beyond question, that this great and powerful institution had been actively engaged in attempting to influence the election of the public officers with its money."

- President Andrew Jackson, 1828 reference to 2nd Central Bank

History has also told us that politicians that challenge the United States privately owned Federal Reserve Central Banking System, or as in the case of President Lincoln, refuse to give in to the "money changers," and in the case of President McKinley, turn on the Capitalists that control the Federal Reserve, they will end up either dead from assassin's bullets or dodging them.

President Jackson   President Lincoln   President McKinley   Louis McFadden

President Jackson pulled out the government's money from the Second Bank of the United States in 1836, and all but dooming the Bank's future. In 1841, the Second Bank of the United States went bankrupt, leaving stockholders, foreign and domestic, empty handed with worthless dollars. On January 30, 1835, at the Capitol Building, Richard Lawrence aimed two flintlock pistols at the President, but both misfired. Lawrence was found not guilty by reason of insanity and confined to a mental institution until his death in 1861.

President Lincoln in 1861 was faced with financing the Civil War with little money. He went out to secure loans, but the best he could do are loans costing 24% to 35% interest, so he rejected their expensive offers. Lincoln got some laws passed and had $450 million of interest-free "Greenbacks" printed. Lincoln's shunning of the money institutions such as the House of Rothschild in England and other loan sharks within the banking institutions, worldwide, all but sealed his own fate.

President McKinley presidencial campaigns were well financed by industrialist Marcus Hanna and John D. Rockefeller. During McKinley's first term, he raised tariffs on imports as high as 57%, which eliminated most foreign competition in goods and services. With little foreign competition, capitalists would charge top dollar for their products and services while reaping increased profits for the industrial and finacial empires. After winning re-election, McKinley had a change of heart towards foreign trade and protecting domestic businesses with high tariffs. President McKinley on September 5th, 1901 at the Pan American Exposition in Buffalo, New York delivered a speech on his new positions on tariffs and trade, which was to lower tariff rates and be more open to new trade agreements, and much to the dislike of his past financial, big-business backers that most benefited financially from high tariff rates. On the second day at the Exposition, September 6th, President McKinley stood in the Temple of Music greeting people from a line that had formed to shake his hand. Leon Frank Czolgosz approached McKinley and fired two shots which eventually killed him. On September 14th, 1901, McKinley would be pronounced died at 2:15 A.M., his assassin convicted during an eight and a half hour "kangaroo-court style trial" on September 23rd and executed only five weeks later.

Congressman Louis McFadden in 1933 brought formal charges against the Board of Governors of the Federal Reserve Bank system, the Comptroller of the Currency and the Secretary of United States Treasury for numerous criminal acts, including; but not limited to, CONSPIRACY, FRAUD, UNLAWFUL CONVERSION, AND TREASON. Only days after Congressman MacFadden's condemnation of the Federal Reserve, two shots were fired at him from an unknown, would-be assassin as he exited a car and walked toward a Washington D. C. hotel. Then weeks later while attending a political banquet, MacFadden fell violently ill from what later was discovered poisoning. His life was spared by a physician attending the banquet procured a stomach pump and gave the Congressman emergency treatment. He would die in 1936 on a visit to New York City of sudden heart failure after being diagnosed with a suspicious intestinal ailment.

The assassination attempt and Business Plot to overthrow President Franklin D. Roosevelt was a forwarning to him not to make good on challenging the United States Federal Reserve privately owned Central Banking System.

"In politics, nothing happens by accident. If it happens, you can bet it was planned that way."
- President Franklin D. Roosevelt

Candidate for president, Franklin D. Roosevelt blamed the Federal Reserve irresponsible handling of America's money as reason for the country falling into the "Great Depression." Many believed he had plans to eliminate the country's Federal Reserve Central Banking System. After the Assassination attempt on his life only days before taking office, and the "Business Plot" to take over the government and throw him out of office was exposed, President Roosevelt had a change of heart towards eliminating the Federal Reserve and the powers behind it.

President John F. Kennedy takes steps to put the United States Federal Reserve Central Banking System OUT OF BUSINESS with Executive Order #11110

Making him the target to those owning the Federal Reserve Central Banking System

Executive Order # 11110 was signed on June 4th, 1963 by President Kennedy that gave the Treasury Department the power "to issue silver certificates against any silver bullion, silver, or standard silver dollars in the Treasury." United States Silver Certificates were issued as an interest-free and debt-free currency backed by silver reserves in the U.S. Treasury, unlike the worthless Federal Reserve Notes issued from the private central bank with no backing, with interest charged and debt accumulating.

Kennedy's plan was within six years, silver certificates would replace all Federal Reserve Notes and the $750 plus million National Debt be paid off. More than $4 billion in United States Silver Certificates were brought into circulation in $2 and $5 denominations. $10 and $20 United States Silver Certificates were never circulated but were being printed by the Treasury Department when Kennedy was assassinated.

President Kennedy knew the Federal Reserve Notes being used as legal currency were contrary to the Constitution of the United States. For the United States taxpayers to pay a privately owned Federal Reserve Central Bank interest for the use of their country's own money was wasting money, unconstitutional and a creation of 12 of the most pro-business, pro-republican, wealthy and powerful people in the United States, Germany and England who gained ownership in the Federal Reserve.

Chapter XII
November 21st, 1963 Conspiracy All Set To Go

Madeleine Duncan Brown Story

Madeleine Brown first spoke publicly in the 1980s of her 21 year relationship with President Lyndon B. Johnson. She claimed they spawned a son together, but more shockingly, said Johnson told her the night before President Kennedy was assassinated, and on his way out of a closed door meeting, that *"After tomorrow, those SOB's, (Kennedys) will never embarrass me again!"*

Brown says she and Johnson attended a party in Dallas hosted by business tycoon and member of the "Suite 8F Group," Clint Murchison. Those present at the event included J. Edgar Hoover & Clyde Tolson of the FBI, John J. McCloy of the CIA, Jack Ruby, George Brown (of Brown and Root), numerous mafia kingpins and Richard Nixon.

Madeleine Duncan Brown in 2002   H.L. Hunt   J. Edgar Hoover & Clyde Tolson

Johnson was still irate when he called Madeleine Brown the morning of the assassination, telling her *"the Irish mafia* (meaning the Kennedy family) *would never embarrass him again."*

Dwight Eisenhower's statement to his brother
"There are a group of well financed and powerful Texans with influential friends through out our country and within governmental agencies that wish to change America's way of life as we know it and will do anything to get their way." **- President Eisenhower, February 1961**

More importantly than him being a part of the Suite F8 Group, is Johnson's close ties with those within the elite financial community. Along with oil millionaire H.L. Hunt, another of Lyndon Johnson's biggest political contributors was **Brown & Root, who in 1963 was owned by Halliburton** and **Brother Brothers & Harriman Company,** who's employees and investors over the years included Prescott & George Bush Sr., George

Herbert Walker, CIA Director Allen Dulles and brother Foster Dulles, Secretary of State to President Eisenhower. Johnson for over two decades steered government projects in the tens-of-millions to people he personally knew and liked, including **Brown & Root** and **Brown Brothers & Harriman Company.**

H.L. Hunt

H.L. Hunt's office was in the building adjacent to the Texas Book Depository where witnesses believed sounds of gun shots came from. Hunt was close friends to David Rockefeller and Texas oilman George W. Bush Sr.

H.L. Hunt, and his son Ray Hunt.   Prescott Bush & his son George & G.W. Bush.

Note: H.L. Hunt's son, Ray, inherited most of his father's Hunt Oil Company that in 2006 was worth over $4 billion. Ray would become a major backer of George & G.W. Bush's runs for president and John McCain for the Senate and President. He would donate $36 million to build the President George W. Bush Library. Ray would serve on the Board of Directors of Halliburton during the Iraq War. In 2007, Ray's Hunt Oil Company signed oil exploration contracts with the Kurds in Iraq only after informing the United States Officials in Iraq, the State Department and the Bush Administration of their impending deal with the Kurdish people.

Ray Hunt

CEO of Hunt Oil 1976-present

Board of Directors member Bessemer Venture Partners, Dresser Industries, EDS, Federal Reserve Bank of Dallas, Halliburton, King Ranch, Pepsi Cola, Verde Reality, American Petroleum Institute and Dallas Petroleum Club. Appointed by President G.W. Bush to the Foreign Intelligence Advisory Board in 2001.

Hunt Oil money has always backed the Bushs campaigns for election to political office as well back Senator McCain of Arizona.

Ray Lee Hunt served on the Committees to elect John McCain to the Senate and Presidency as well as on Committees to both George Bush Sr. and G.W. Bush's into their campaigns into an assortment of political offices.

President G.W. Bush when asked of the Hunt Oil contracts with the Kurds would resort to the "Bush Family line" of not knowing anything about it...a pattern lasting

three generations when Bush Family members when asked question that truthful answers would incriminate themselves of being apart of criminal activity from Prescott Bush have no knowledge that the Union Bank of New York which he was Director and ran the bank said he didn't know the bank was helping Nazi Germany and when Vice-President George Bush Sr. Said he knew nothing of the CIA's involvement in South America or America selling poison gas to Iraq to be used on the Iranians even though his signature was on the papers that authorize the sale. George's mind goes blank when asked why was he standing inform of the Texas Book Depository minutes after President Kennedy was Assassinated, only saying "I don't remember where I was the day JFK was assassinated." George would lie to Congress during hearings to confirm his appointment to the office of Director of the CIA by saying he had never worked for the CIA, by which admitting his involvement FBI Director J. Edgar Hoover's letter exposed him as, would of connected his involvement to the Invasion of Cuba and very possibly lead to him or his father Prescott's involvement to assassinating President John F. Kennedy.

Disinformation

Although one may think it was the Suite F8 Group that were the *Powers Behind JFK Assassination,* and in truth, some of the members were called on to help with the planning, assassination and cover up, but were only lower level conspirators. They believed the Kennedy Assassination was payback for President Kennedy not backing CIA Director's invasion of Cuba with air support. It would be one of many disinformation stories the CIA would leak out to divert the public's attention from the truth Stories of mafia ties to Joseph Kennedy, President Kennedy's affairs with mob boss' mistress, broken deals the Kennedy's made with the mafia, Castro of Cuba ordering the hit on Kennedy, Russia did it and dozens of other conspiracy theories would server those real *Powers Behind JFK Assassination* well to confuse the public.

Much has been made out of President Kennedy's plans to pull out of Vietnam was reason for his Assassination, but history has told us other presidents had ended wars and military conflicts but were not assassinated. But without question, President Kennedy would of ended the United States involvement in Vietnam within a couple of years, if not sooner.

Historians continue to debate whether Kennedy was serious on pulling out of Vietnam without looking at the entire picture. President Kennedy's Executive Order #11110 that not only would of put the "privately owned" Federal Reserve out of business with is silver back interest free Silver Certificates and eliminated the National Debt, but would of force the United States to have a balanced budget; which any involvement of war in Vietnam would of made a balanced budget impossible.

Chapter XIII
November 22nd, 1963

Did History Repeating Itself?

"The government should create, issue and circulate all of its currency and credit to satisfy the spending power of the government and the buying power of consumers...The privilege of creating and issuing money is not only a supreme prerogative of government, but it is the government's greatest creative opportunity... By the adoption of these principles, the taxpayers will save immense sums of interest...Money will cease to be master, and become servant to humanity." -President Abraham Lincoln

"If this mischievous financial policy, which has it's origin in North America, shall become indurate down to a fixture, then that government will furnish it's own money without cost. It will payoff debts, and go without debt. It will have all the money necessary to carry on its commerce. It will become prosperous without precedent in the history of the world. The brains and wealth of all countries will all go to America. That country must be destroyed, or it will destroy every monarchy in the world." – London Newspaper

Looking at Connally, is this a man wondering when the shooting will begin?

Was Kennedy feeling the heat from the Federal Reserve?

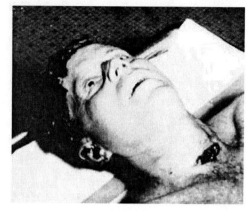

"The high office of the President has been used to foment a plot to destory America's freedoms, and before I leave office, I must inform the citizens of his plight."

\- President Kennedy

"The greated danger to the freedoms and way of life for the citizens of the United States is not the Soviet Union or Communist China, but the National Debt."
\- President John F. Kennedy

Then it started!

President Kennedy's car is past Texas Book Depository

NOTE: In the second car, Secret Service men, driver and passenger in front seat, along with front man standing on the car's step board to the right and next to the driver, have their attention on front car that President Kennedy is in. Secret Service man without sunglasses standing on step board behind front man has his attention on the two Secret Service men standing on step board on the other side of car, whose attention is back toward entrance of Texas Book Depository. A closer look at the picture is needed.

Also notice the tree to the left of the motorcade. The tree are filled with leafs, and would block the view of any shot from the 6th floor of the Texas Book Depository until the motorcade drove farther away. The first shot came from the adjacent building housing H. L. Hunt's Office.

Hey! Some guy is wearing Lee Oswald's shirt (circled)?

Good to see Lee Oswald got his shirt back!

Many have claimed the picture of the man at the front door to the book depository was a different employee wearing an identical shirt and t-shirt as Lee Oswald. FBI's only picture of such employee was taken 13 years after the Assassination that does hold a resemblance to Oswald, but wearing a similar shirt that he was wearing that day. Also, said employee's boss to the FBI, "it couldn't have been him because he was sitting at my feet eating lunch when motorcade passed by the Texas Book Depository."

1st Shot from H.L. Hunt's Office Building, adjacent from the Texas Book Depository

President Kennedy has reacted to being shot and Mrs. Kennedy has noticed. Surely the time for the Kennedys to react wasn't faster than a bullet leaving the President and hitting Governor Connally, who seems not hit or aware of what is going on. Could President Kennedy been shot, felt the burning and lifted his arms faster than the speed of a bullet leaving his body to Connally?

So much for the Gerald Ford-Allen Spector "single bullet theory."

United States House of Representatives Select Committee on Assassinations
Testimony of Dr. Cyril H.Wecht, Coroner, Allegheny County, PA.

Chairman STOKES. You may be seated. The Chair recognizes staff counsel, Donald A. Purdy, Jr.

Mr. PURDY. Thank you, Mr. Chairman…Dr. Wecht, did you request to testify today?

Dr. WECHT. Yes, I did.

Mr. PURDY. Dr. Wecht, what are the major conclusions of the forensic pathology panel with which you are in disagreement?

Dr. WECHT. The major disagreement is the single-bullet theory which I deem to be the very essence of the Warren Commission report's conclusions and all the other corroborating panels and groups since that time. It is the sine qua non of the Warren Commission report's conclusions vis-a-vis a sole assassin. Without the single-bullet theory, there cannot be one assassin, whether it is Oswald or anybody else. I am in disagreement with various other conclusions of the panel. I am most unhappy and have been extremely dismayed by their failure to insist upon the performance of appropriate experiments, which I believe could have been undertaken with a reasonable degree of expenditure of time, energy, and money to once and for all show whether a bullet 6.5-millimeter, copper-jacketed, lead core piece of military-type ammunition could indeed strike a rib and a radius in a human being and emerge in the condition which Commission exhibit 399 is today. I am extremely unhappy about the fact that a greater and more intensive effort was not made to locate the missing pieces of very important medical evidence in this case, which I pointed out back in the summer of 1972. Not that I was the first to learn of this, but amazingly, nobody had made that public disclosure prior to that time. I have raised same questions concerning the head wound and the possibility, albeit remote, of a second shot fired in synchronized fashion from the right side or the lower right rear, synchronized with the head shot that struck the President in the back of the head. And this is related to a few pieces, a couple of pieces of evidence and, again, emphasizes the necessity of having the brain to examine. These are the major areas. There are, of course, numerous facets of all of these disagreements that are related to the so-called single-bullet theory.

Mr. PURDY. Dr. Wecht, is it your opinion that no bullet could have caused all of the wounds to President Kennedy and Governor Connally or the Commission exhibit 399 could not have caused all of the wounds to both men?

Dr. WECHT. Based upon the findings in this case, it is my opinion that no bullet could have caused all these wounds, not only 399 but no other bullet that we know about or any fragment of any bullet that we know about in this case.

Mr. PURDY. Dr. Wecht, what point along the film do you feel corresponds with the time when President Kennedy and Governor Connally were ,supposed to have been hit, according to the single bullet theory?

Dr. WECHT. Commission exhibit of--I am sorry--an exhibit of this panel, of this committee, of 229, which is a blow-up of Zapruder frame 193, demonstrates the President and Governor Connally just before they go in behind the Stemmons Freeway sign. Both gentlemen are turned to the right facing the crowd and their right arms are extended in a

162

wave of greeting or recognition. This exhibit F-272, is a blowup of Zapruder frame 222 and shows Gov. John Connally after emergence from behind the Stemmons Freeway sign, and F-244, which is a blowup of Zapruder frame 225, shows the President and Gov. John Connally. In my opinion, Zapruder frame 193 clearly demonstrates that neither gentlemen had been shot.

Mr. PURDY. Wecht, based on F-229, what is the basis for your opinion that neither man had been struck by a bullet in that photograph?

Dr. WECHT. There is absolutely no external physical manifestation, no reaction of any kind on their part of a voluntary or involuntary nature which would even suggest they have been struck by a missile.

Mr. PURDY. Dr. Wecht, is it possible that either or both men have been struck by a bullet but are not yet manifesting a reaction?

Dr. WECHT. In my opinion, without any question, no.

The bullet found at Parkland Hospital

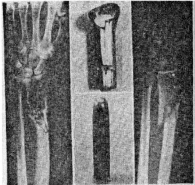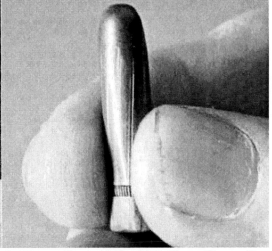

WHEN A BULLET like the one that hit Gov. John Connally was test-fired into a cadaver's wristbone (X-ray at left) its tip was severely flattened (bullet shown at top.) But the lower bullet, which the Warren Commission says wounded President Kennedy and the governor is nearly perfect in contour. X-ray of Connally's wrist is shown at right.

(Above) When a bullet like wrist bone the one that hit Gov. Connally was test fired into a cadaver's, its tip was severely flattened.
Doctors recovered bits and pieces of the bullet shot into Governor Connally, but the bullet that is claimed to have went thru President Kennedy and into Gov. Connally damaging his wrist, (right), has no pieces missing and almost in perfect condition. So how could it be the same bullet that hit Connally if no pieces are missing? Where did the bullet fragments taken from Connally come from, unless there was another bullet, another shot taken, and a second shooter from behind.

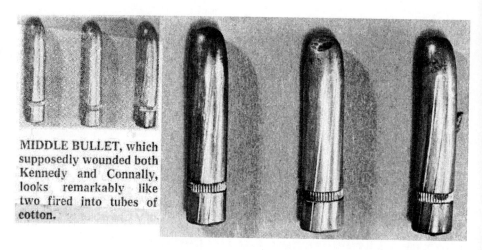

MIDDLE BULLET, which supposedly wounded both Kennedy and Connally, looks remarkably like two fired into tubes of cotton.

From the curved marking on the side of the bullet, all three were shot from the same rifle. But when could of the so called "magic bullet" been fired from the gun? They could not have after the assassination, thus only leaving the time prior to the assassination on November 22nd of 1963 to create evidence. The fact that the bullet found at Parkland Hospital and was shot from the rifle found in the Texas Book Depository is enough evidence to prove a conspiracy, since Oswald couldn't of place the bullet in the Hospital. Logic would also say, the "magic bullet" was fired from the rifle before November 22nd, 1963 and recovered by someone other than Oswald...thus, someone else must of entered the Paine garage before November 22nd, 1963, taken the rifle to a place where they could fire and recover the bullet, then return the gun to the garage...this is proof of not only a conspiracy, but Oswald being framed.

2nd Shot from the Texas Book Depository

Now look at the picture closer and add the words Connally yelled.

164

"My God, they are going to kill us all!"

If I were shot, I would think my 1st words would be "I'm shot!" Using the words "...they are going to kill us all!" would make one think Connally had someone in mine as to who is doing the shooting. Since Vice-President Johnson knew about the Assassination the day before, and Connally was member of the Suite F8 Group, he probably also knew about the planned hit on President Kennedy too.

3rd Shot, from the Texas Book Depository missed its target and hit a curb, splashing debris and bullet fragment onto bystander, United States Air Force Veteran James Tague

James Tague got out of his car and was standing for two to three seconds near the Dealey Plaza south curbstone of Main Street, 520 feet (158 m) southwest from the Texas School Book Depository and a few feet east of the eastern edge of the triple overpass railroad bridge, when Tague saw the presidential limousine, then he heard the first shot. Tague stated that some gunfire came from the direction of the grassy knoll.

Right after the shots ended and the motorcade left for Parkland Hospital, Tague was approached by a Dallas police detective who immediately noticed that Tague had specks of blood on his right facial cheek. (Tague also had a small left facial scab, but it had happened several days before the attack.) The two men examined the area to discover on the upper curve of the Main Street south curbstone, a "very fresh scar" impact that, to each of them, looked like a bullet had struck there and taken a chip out of the curbstone concrete. (The curb surrounding the scar chip was not cut out by investigators until August 1964 and is now in the National Archives.) The scar chip was 23 feet 6 inches (7.2 m) east of the east edge of the Triple Underpass railroad bridge, about 20 (6.1 m) feet from where Tague stood during the attack. The detective told Tague it looked like a bullet had been fired from one of the Houston or Elm streets intersection buildings and had struck there. The detective then radioed-in that information to the police dispatcher at the same time that a large group of witnesses and authorities were running towards and searching the grassy knoll and railroad parking lot adjacent to the grassy knoll.

4th Shot from Behind Fence
Kills President John F. Kennedy

The final shot from the front was an exploding bullet at impact, unlike the first three bullets fired from behind President Kennedy. No bullet would be recovered from the final shot, only a bent shell casing setting on the ledge of the fence that someone's teeth had bitten into. James Files claimed to have bitten into the shell casing after shooting President Kennedy years before the Dallas Police Department revealed the bent shell casing evidence to the public.

Looks like (CIA Agent) George H.W. Bush Sr. made it to Dallas, (circled).

Dallas Police Officers seal off the Book Depository Building.

Notice how the crowd has been cleared away except for police and Bush. The only reason George W. Bush Sr. would have been allowed to stand there is if he flashed his CIA Identification. Also note, Bush is no where in sight before the shooting in picture of motorcade on pages 156-7.

Not sure? Take another look.

Is George Bush Sr. in all three photos?

Information kept from the public eyes until October 15th, 1993, is a memorandum from Special Agent of the FBI Graham Kitchel (next page), SAC FBI office in Houston, Texas. Agent Kitchel's memorandum conveys a discussion he had with a Mr. GEORGE H.W. BUSH, who identified himself as President of Zapata Off-Shore Oil Drilling Company, Houston, Texas and wanted their conversation kept confidential.

UNITED STATES GOVERNMENT

Memorandum

TO   :   SAC, HOUSTON   DATE;   11-22-63

FROM :   SA GRAHAM W. KITCHEL

SUBJECT: UNKNOWN SUBJECT;
ASSASSINATION OF PRESIDENT
JOHN F. KENNEDY

At 1:45 p.m. Mr. GEORGE H. W. BUSH, President
of the Zapata Off-shore Drilling Company, Houston, Texas,
residence 5525 Briar, Houston, telephonically furnished
the following information to writer by long distance
telephone call from Tyler, Texas.

BUSH stated that he wanted to be kept confidential
but wanted to furnish hearsay that he recalled hearing in
recent weeks, the day and source unknown. He stated that
one JAMES PARROTT has been talking of killing the President
when he comes to Houston.

BUSH stated that PARROTT is possibly a student
at the University of Houston and is active in political
matters in this area. He stated that he felt Mrs. PARLEY,
telephone number SU 2-5239, or ARLINE SMITH, telephone
number JA 9-9194 of the Harris County Republican Party
Headquarters would be able to furnish additional information regarding the identity of PARROTT.

BUSH stated that he was proceeding to Dallas, Texas,
would remain in the Sheraton-Dallas Hotel and return to his
residence on 11-23-63. His office telephone number is
CA 2-0395.

ALL INFORMATION CONTAINED
HEREIN IS UNCLASSIFIED
DATE 10-15-93 BY 9803 AJO/HSR
(JFK)

GWK:djw
(2) djw

Schmidt -

graham

62-2115-6

SEARCHED____ INDEXED____
SERIALIZED 2214 FILED 20
NOV 16 1963
FBI - HOUSTON

NOTE: One must keep in mind when reading this United States Government, SAC Memorandum, (previous page), is dated November 22, 1963, about a discussion that happened at 1:45pm, over 90 minutes after President Kennedy was shot. The only George H.W. Bush (H.W. standing for Herbert Walker, George Bush's marital grandfather), owning Zapata Company is the future Ambassador to the United Nations that at the time got the then Bush close family friend President Nixon to side with the communist wing of China and was instrumental as the United States representative to begin trading with Communist China under President Nixon, Director of the CIA appointed by also close Bush family friend President Ford, Vice President under President Ronald Reagan and President of the United States; and the same "Zapata Company" that CIA Agents among themselves called "Operation 40" for "The Bay of Pigs Operation," "Operation Zapata."

This same George H.W. Bush is the one FBI Director J. Edgar Hoover in a letter from his desk, (below) dated only seven days after the Kennedy Assassination, November 29th, 1963, identify him as a CIA Agent and "informant who furnished reliable information in the past," pertaining to the pro-Castro & anti-Castro Cuban community. Information within the letter was given to J. Edgar Hoover "orally furnished by Mr. George Bush of the Central Intelligence Agency," which means he spoke with George Bush in person or by telephone within days of the Kennedy Assassination, for whatever other reasons.

And the same George H. W. Bush since President Kennedy's Assassination that claims in public that he can't remember where he was or what he was doing on the day Kennedy was assassinated.

George H. W. Bush is the grand son of Globalist, well known industrialist and member of the Board of Directors and major stockholder of the Federal Reserve in Cleveland, Ohio, Samuel Bush. Since Samuel, Bush Family has been Globalists, retained their stock in the Federal Reserve for four generations and would do anything to protect their own and close family friend and business associates for four generations, the Rockefeller Family's interest and ownership in the Federal Reserve.

November 29, 1963

To: Director
        Bureau of Intelligence and Research
        Department of State

From: John Edgar Hoover, Director

Subject: ASSASSINATION OF PRESIDENT JOHN F. KENNEDY
          NOVEMBER 22, 1963

          Our Miami, Florida, Office on November 23, 1963, advised
that the Office of Coordinator of Cuban Affairs in Miami advised
that the Department of State feels some misguided anti-Castro
group might capitalize on the present situation and undertake an
unauthorized raid against Cuba, believing that the assassination
of President John F. Kennedy might herald a change in U. S. policy,
which is not true.

          Our sources and informants familiar with Cuban matters in
the Miami area advise that the general feeling in the anti-Castro
Cuban community is one of stunned disbelief and, even among those
who did not entirely agree with the President's policy concerning
Cuba, the feeling is that the President's death represents a great
loss not only to the U. S. but to all of Latin America. These
sources knew of no plans for unauthorized action against Cuba.

          An informant who has furnished reliable information in
the past and who is close to a small pro-Castro group in Miami
has advised that these individuals are afraid that the assassination
of the President may result in strong repressive measures being
taken against them and, although pro-Castro in their feelings,
regret the assassination.

          The substance of the foregoing information was orally
furnished to Mr. George Bush of the Central Intelligence Agency and
Captain William Edwards of the Defense Intelligence Agency on
November 23, 1963, by Mr. W. T. Forsyth of this Bureau.

          1 - Director of Naval Intelligence

DEC-36 62-109060-1396

After carefully reading the previous letters from the FBI Director J. Edgar Hoover in Washington D.C. and Office of the FBI in Houston, Texas, one must wonder why they had been kept from the public's eyes for so long. Secondly, why didn't George Herbert Walker Bush Sr. say something about his contact with the Miami anti-Castro Cubans or of his phone call to a FBI Office to the Warren Commission or any of the following commissions investigating the JFK Assassination? The only reason would be, is that Bush had something to hide. THINK ABOUT IT!

Pertaining to the FBI memorandum dated the day of the JFK Assassination at 1:45pm regarding a telephone call received from George Bush Sr. one would have to wonder why Bush made the call. Had it been James Parrott who shot Kennedy, Bush as a CIA Agent would have been blamed for not reporting it to his bosses, the FBI or Secret Service in the weeks before the Assassination when he first heard of it. The world would have blamed CIA Agent George W. H. Bush Sr. for not reporting what he had heard weeks ago; especially since Bush had a name to the story of assassinating President Kennedy.

The reader must keep in mind, that in 1963, not only those threatening to, or speaking of assassinating, the President of the United States would have gotten FBI and/or Secret Service Agents knocking on their door for questioning and possible arrest, but this was a time FBI Agents were investigating citizens for leading protests against the Vietnam War or racial discrimination. Surely, had George Bush passed on his information before the JFK Assassination, both FBI and Secret Service Agents would have been all over this James Parrot, including knocking on his door. And CIA Agent George H. W. Bush knew that.

So why did CIA Agent George H. W. Bush make the call? From his father, Prescott Bush, and George Bush's past CIA boss & family close friend Allen Dulles, George Bush definitely was told about the assassination before it took place, if not a player in it.

The letter also said George H. W. Bush Sr. said he was calling from Tyler, Texas. Because of Bush's silence on the matter and no record of him testifying to it, there is also no record of the FBI checking their phone records to verify that George Bush was in fact calling from Tyler, Texas. If George Bush really was calling from Tyler, Texas, one can only come to the conclusion that Bush's telephone call was to give himself an alibi during the JFK Assassination? THINK ABOUT IT. CIA Agent George H. W. Bush was standing in front of the Texas Book Depository minutes after President Kennedy's Assassination, then drives to Tyler, Texas to make a telephone call to an FBI Office in Houston, Texas. And because George Bush Sr. knew about the assassination beforehand, he would also know who was behind it; which means Bush's telephone call was not only for his alibi, but also to mislead an investigation by the FBI from the real shooter to James Parrott.

172

NOTE: As an average citizen of the United States, you may be saying to yourself George Bush's actions are too much to take…and I would agree with you if George Bush Sr. on November of 1963 wasn't a CIA Agent, BUT GEORGE BUSH SR. WAS ONE AT THE TIME; according to FBI Director J. Edgar Hoover's letter…and this is what CIA Agents did when toppling a government. The reason our government waited till 1993, 30 years after the assassination, to de-classify the letter about George Bush's telephone to the FBI only 90 minutes after the shooting is because with the previously released letter from FBI Director J. Edgar Hoover's desk ties George Bush Sr. into the JFK Assassination; if only as someone knowing about it beforehand.

UNFORTUNATELY FOR THE TRUTH, BUSH CLAIMS HE CAN'T REMEMBER WHAT HE DID THAT DAY!

Thus, George Herbert Walker Bush Sr. becomes the only man in the United States that this author has talked with in the 45 years since the Assassination that can't remember what they were doing the day President Kennedy was MURDERED!

Chapter XIV
Conspiracy, Opportunity, Motive & Pattern

George de Mohrenschildt

No one person was more connected with the Kennedy Assassination on both sides than CIA & FBI, unknowingly at the time, pawn George de Mohrenschildt.

He had closed friendships with Jackie Kennedy and her family, George and Prescott Bush, H. Howard Hunt, Rockefellers and closest friend to Lee Oswald.

In later years, George admitted to Willem Otlmam of Dutch TV that he unknowingly helped to manipulate Lee Oswald for the CIA into the plot to assassinate President Kennedy.

De Mohrenschildt was Russian, college professor, a member of the Petroleum Club with George H.W. Bush Sr. and a well known, respected international geologist with friendships at the highest spectrum of wealth, power and influence. This is, until he began talking to the media about his activates surrounding players and witnesses to President Kennedy's Assassination.

After de Mohrenschildt complained to his friend, the then CIA Director George Bush Sr. that he was under surveillance and being harassed by CIA Agents, Bush talked with FBI Director J. Edgar Hoover and George de Mohrenschildt was unwillingly committed to Parkland Hospital. Over a short period of time there, George was given nine electroconvulsive shock treatments. The treatments would, for periods of time during the rest of his life, disoriented George. With a history of being committed as a Psychological Ward at Parkland Hospital on his record, it became useful information to discredited him on anything he said about the JFK Assassination, players and witnesses he came in contact with prior to and after the Assassination.

Little did the conspirators know at the time, that de Mohrenschildt had, previous to his shock treatments, written a manuscript and had been taped by Dutch TV to all that he

174

knew of President Kennedy's Assassination and his actions involving naming players and witnesses to the crime of the 20th Century.

On March 29, 1977, while on a break from an interview, de Mohrenschildt received a card from Gaeton Fonzi, an investigator for the House Select Committee on Assassinations, that he would be called to testify. That afternoon he committed suicide by shooting himself in the mouth with a shotgun.

Conspiracy

Conspiracy by definition is "an evil, unlawful plan formulated in secret by two or more people; a plot."

Without question President Kennedy's Assassination was planned, carried out and covered up by two or more people, which by definition is a **conspiracy.**

Proof of a conspiracy is not only from the condition of the bullet found at Parkland Hospital as clearly explained on previous pages, eye witnesses and the Zapruder Film of the Assassination tell and show, respectively, bullets came from more than one direction. Thus with more than one shooter, by definition President Kennedy's Assassination was carried out by **conspiracy.**

Opportunity

Opportunity depended on the shooter's accessibility to President Kennedy, which on November 22nd, 1963 turned out to be easily attained in Dealey Plaza.

Opportunity of those *Powers Behind JFK Assassination* was their access to people with expertise to carry out the assassination before President Kennedy's Executive Order #11110 became fully implemented. Since the Bush Family retained Samuel Bush's stock holdings in the Federal Reserve Bank in Cleveland, they had much to lose had Executive Order #11110 continued. The Bush Family's past business and personnel dealings with x-CIA Director Allen Dulles and George Bush Sr. being a CIA Agent at the time, they had access to professional assassins; thus **opportunity to arrange and hire those to plan and carry out the Assassination.**

Motive

Motive is the easiest to prove and explain...**MONEY and CONTROL OVER THE LARGEST POOL OF MONEY IN THE WORLD!** Had President Kennedy lived, his Executive Order #11110 would have put the Federal Reserve out of business within six years as well as pay off the national debt. Kennedy already had the United States Treasury Department distribute millions of Silver Certificates in two-dollar and five-dollar denominations while ten-dollar and twenty-dollar Silver Certificates were being made at the time of his death. Executive Order #11110 would have cost the Bush Family, the Rockefellers, the Rothschilds, the Warburgs and all other owners of the

Federal Reserve billions of dollars in future profits. These Globalist owners of the Federal Reserve would have also lost excess to huge low interest loans to expand their own business interests in industry and financial institutions as well as worldwide influence they attained by owning and controlling the largest pool of money in the world.

Pattern

For over two centuries, United States citizens, presidents and congressmen have debated, argued, and feared for their life, against those wealthy Globalists doing anything to attain, than keep control of the United States currency. The first two attempts at a United States "privately owned" central banking system ended in failure while all but bankrupting the United States government. In both cases, the president at the time pulled out what little of the government's money was left from the Central Bank.

One of those presidents, Andrew Jackson, had at least twice escaped assassination attempts. But one president wasn't so lucky and died from an assassin's bullet after he rejected offers from the wealthy capitalist "money changers," and as President Kennedy would do in the future, Abraham Lincoln had the United States Treasury Department print, distribute and regulate the country's currency. Once in the 1930's, a congressman filed charges against those irresponsible owners, directors and employees of the Federal Reserve for fraud and theft, among an assortment of other charges, only to be dodging would be assassin's bullets days later. This same congressman, weeks later would escape sure death from poisoning during a party if it hadn't been for a doctor standing by and pumped out his stomach. He would years later die of stomach complications.

Also in the 1930's, President-elect Roosevelt narrowly escaped an assassin's gun fire after threatening to abolish the corrupt Federal Reserve "privately owned" Central Bank once in the White House. Then once in office survived the famous "Business Plot" to throw him out of office by force. This "Plot" was devised and carried out, before being caught and stopped, by some of the very people that owned the Federal Reserve.

One successful presidential assassination came to a President McKinley that had turned on his wealthy financial backers after he once got re-elect to a second term. He spoke of lowering import-tariffs and opening trade to other countries by changing the country's trade policies that had protected his financial, elitist backers that had controlled and manipulated their markets.

The pattern for over two centuries is clear. **CHALLENGING the FEDERAL RESERVE "PRIVATLY OWNED" CENTRAL BANKING SYSTEM WILL MAKE YOUR LIFE EXPENDABLE.**

Chapter XV
Players

Assassins

Assassins for Kennedy's Assassination were definitely at the bottom of the food chain and were assassinated themselves shortly thereafter or locked away in a prison for life so that they could only tell one of the planned disinformation stories unrelated to the Federal Reserve. The three pawn-assassin teams knew no one else within the conspiracy except their handler, including members of the other pawn-assassin teams. The pawn-assassins were hired guns by the then x-CIA Director Allen Dulles that had used them before.

Note: Over the years an array of professional and amateur assassins are linked to Kennedy's Assassination. Some of the assassins might have taken credit for something they had planned to do, but failed. Or evidence put them in position to look as though they were a part of the Assassination for purpose of either using them for disinformation, or using them for a previous planned Assassination of Kennedy. Evidence has shown the Kennedy Assassination was first planned to take place weeks earlier in Chicago, in Miami and finally the *Powers Behind JFK Assassination* accomplish their goal in Dallas, Texas.

Handlers

Handlers were experience CIA Agents, some active and others not. They were loyal to Allen Dulles, Richard Bissell and Charles Cabell, who were forced to resign after their planned *Bay of Pigs* invasion failed. They knew nothing of the larger conspiracy or real reason for the "hit," only that they were paying Kennedy back for forcing their bosses to resign and not standing by them during the *Bay of Pigs* invasion with air support. The handler's responsibilities were to position their pawn-assassin at their post for the assassination. The handlers only told members of their pawn-assassin the name of the person they were to hit seconds before the shooting began so that it would be too late for them to back out, and if the assassination was aborted at the last second they would not know who was about to be assassinated.

Their patsy, Lee Harvey Oswald, was in-part put together by an unknowingly handler George de Mohrenschildt. George's handler could have been more than one person including old friend and CIA Agent George Bush Sr. and/or his father Prescott Bush.

The handlers knew one another and their director, but no one other than that in the conspiracy. Their responsibilities also included to cleaning up after the Assassination by assassinating or getting someone to kill the shooters and untrusting witnesses. E. Howard Hunt and Cord Meyer were just two of them who's job it was to make sure evidence to the crime got no farther than the assassins.

Directors

Directors were those with years of experience and vast reaches world wide to contract professional assassins they had used and trusted in other CIA led assassinations. They too had limited knowledge of who were involved and why they were setting up a hit on the president of the United States. They too also believed it was pay back against Kennedy for them losing their jobs at the CIA and not fully backing their plans of invading Cuba. Allen Dulles, Richard Bissell and Charles Cabell all lost their jobs and had grudges against President Kennedy and were more than happy to organize and carry out just one more assassination for the sake of justice in their minds, but more like revenge.

When people for decades have organized and carried out assassinations to replace another country's leaders without being caught or being suspected in being involved, as the CIA had done many times since World War II, assassinating President Kennedy was just another day's work for CIA agents Allen Dulles, Richard Bissell, Charles Cabell, Cord Meyer, E. Howard Hunt and other experienced agents.

Link to the Federal Reserve

The link to the owners of the Federal Reserve only knew the names of the head Director to the Assassination, Allen Dulles. Dulles had no knowledge of handlers or pawn-assassins. The link was Prescott Bush, who had ties to Allen Dulles going back decades to when Dulles diverted investigators from Prescott Bush and Brown Brothers Harriman & Company and their involvement in helping Hitler and the Nazis after World War II. The Bush Family also were stockholders in the Federal Reserve, as well as a general dislike for the Kennedy Family and what President Kennedy's Executive Order #11110 was doing to their family interests and their friends that also owned the Federal Reserve, including personal friend and banker, David Rockefeller. John J. McCloy was overseeing the entire operation for David Rockefeller and owners of the Federal Reserve.

Owners of the Federal Reserve Central Banking System

Federal Reserve owners are known today by very few, and in 1963 even less were aware of who they were or even that the Federal Reserve is privately owned.

These owners of the **Federal Reserve** live in a world unfamiliar to the average American. They lived in locked, gated estates with plenty security, swimming pools, tennis courts and private golf courses. They have servants, maids, gardeners and chuffers, dine at only the finest of restaurants and belong to the most exclusive of clubs. Their children attend only the best of private schools and earning a college degree goes without question. They run and own empires in industry, banking and big business domestic and foreign. Their money is handled by accounting firms they own, their over inflated ego is nurtured by huge business dealings that better their neighbors also living in the top one-percent of the wealthy. Because of their wealth, that they could hardly spend in one life time, their business plans included foresight well beyond their own life time.

These **Globalists** plans were for their sons and grandsons; to secure a future path of riches for them and generations beyond with their goal of globalism with free trade.

These owners of the **Federal Reserve** are what us commoners call, **untouchables…**out of touch with what the average American, and **out of the reach of law enforcement.**

The Federal Reserve, it is said, took in almost **ONE TRILLION DOLLARS** in 2007. No telling how many **TENS OF TRILLIONS OF DOLLARS** the Federal Reserve have taken in these past 45 years since the assassination of President John F. Kennedy and President Lyndon B. Johnson began ignoring Executive Order #11110. **President Reagan** would later repeal Executive Order #11110.

The obvious motive for assassination, the **TRILLIONS OF DOLLARS IN PROFIT WOULD BE ONE.** As you have read, there is a clear pattern over the past two centuries; presidents and one congressman who challenged the Federal Reserve's authority to control the United States Currency, ended up dead or dodging bullets.

George Bush Sr. will not talk. Saying he can't remember what he was doing, or where he was at during the time when President Kennedy was assassinated; making him just about the only United States citizen that can't remember. With almost all the participants to the JFK Assassination dead, what George Bush Sr. really knows and why he was in Dallas that day would most likely shed valuable light on the conspiracy. Not only has George Bush Sr. always been silent, but hasn't ever come forward with any information relating to his contact with people directly or indirectly involved in the Assassination, which we know he was as a CIA Agent had to have been in contact with some of them. Congressional Committees following the Warren Report, has criticized both CIA Director Allen Dulles and George W. Bush for holding back.

The fact that Bush would be there in the first place, leads to suspicion, since through his father, Senator Prescott Bush, had arranged for George one-to-one private conversations in the past with Presidents. And what are the odds that George Bush Sr. would choose the one spot in the entire motorcade route that Kennedy would be shot. If CIA Agent George Bush didn't know of the planned assassination, which is unlikely, his father did and probably called him up and told George and he decided to drive over to Dallas to get a front row seat.

Dulles, Cabell and Bissel was forced to resign from their Director jobs at the CIA. Dulles had worked with **Senator Prescott Bush** and **David Rockefeller** over the years and was perfect to organized and direct the JFK Assassination. Allen Dulles had replaced heads of state in many other countries since the end of World War II. Charles Cabell older brother was Dallas, Texas, Mayor, Earle Cabell, so the CIA Assassination foresaw no local interference…and probably allowed Lee Oswald's assassination to take place.

The UNTOUCHABLE OWNERS OF THE FEDERAL RESERVE... In 1963, chances are, less than 1% of the public knew the names of those 12 owners of the Federal Reserve, more or less understand how President Kennedy's Executive Order #11110 would effect the public or its owners. To Kennedy, it was the first step of eliminating the national debt. It was also going to end the reign of 12 bankers from controlling and running the United States Currency System. Within 6 years, the Federal Reserve privately owned Central Banking System would be out of business; no longer controlling the United States credit in businesses and the country's citizens.

Federal Reserve owners had their "endless cash cow" customer, the United States that paid only interest on their country's debt; thus assuring them of payments for eternity. More important to the owners of the Federal Reserve, was the power they would lose from receiving huge loans from the Federal Reserve for the own financial institutions. They then would lend it back to the United States with interest, to other countries to give themselves excess to foreign businesses and government leaders.

FEDERAL RESERVE OWNERS, had President Kennedy lived to see Executive Order #11110 through, would of lost **tens of trillions of dollars; MOTIVE ENOUGH.**

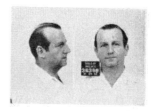

Jacob Rubenstein a.k.a. Jack Leon Ruby
March 25th, 1911 - January 3rd, 1967

When Jack Ruby killed Lee Harvey Oswald, he not only silence an accused assassin, but the truth.

Most legal minds beleive Oswald would of never been convicted in court...although the media all but convicted him shortly after his arrest.

For forty-five years, books and movies have speculated on what really happened and who else was involved with the Assassination of President John F. Kennedy. Few people are alive today that could shed light onto what really happened and who was involved. This book has shed light mostly to why Kennedy had to be assassinated. President Johnson ordered the silver certificates Kennedy was using to end the reign of the privately owned Federal Reserve out of circulation and President Reagan repealed Executive Order #11110.

Much has changed since President Kennedy's Assassination; America lost its innocence and people have little hope as they did in John and Bobby Kennedy's time.

In 2008, the country, our politicians, our trade policies, all that once was America's freedom way of life is either gone or tarnished by those sinful Globalists controlling and owning the Federal Reserve; just as President Kennedy forewarned.

"The high office of the President has been used to foment a plot to destroy the American freedoms, and before I leave office, I must inform the citizens of his plight." - President Kennedy, the *"his plight"* in the above quote was Kennedy speaking of international banker, lifelong globalist, member of the trilateral commission, Chairman of the Bilderberg Invitation Committee and major stockholder of the Federal Reserve, David Rockefeller Sr.

David Rockefeller Sr. explained it best!

"We are grateful to the Washington Post, the New York Times, Time magazine, and other great publications whose directors have attended our meetings and respected their promises of discretion for almost forty years. It would have been impossible for us to develop our plan for the world if we had been subject to the bright lights of publicity during these years. But the world is now more sophisticated and prepared to march towards a world government which will never again know war, but only peace and prosperity for the whole of humanity. The supranational sovereignty of an intellectual elite and world bankers is surely preferable to the national auto determination practiced in the past centuries. It is also our duty to inform the press of our convictions as to the historic future of the century."
- David Rockefeller Sr., Bilderberg meeting in Baden-Baden, Germany, 1991

"For more than a century, ideological extremists at either end of the political spectrum have seized upon well-publicized incidents such as my encounter with Castro to attack the Rockefeller family for the inordinate influence they claim we wield over American political and economic institutions. Some even believe we are part of a secret cabal working against the best interests of the United States, characterizing my family and me as 'internationalists' and of conspiring with others around the world to build a more integrated global political and economic structure — one world, if you will. If that is the charge, I stand guilty, and I am proud of it."

- From David Rockefeller's "Memoirs", (p.405).

David Rockefeller, is the youngest and only surviving child and grandchild, respectively, of the prominent John D. Rockefeller, Jr. and the billionaire oil tycoon John D. Rockefeller, founder of Standard Oil…Standard Oil was forced under anti-monopoly laws to break up into 34 smaller companies, which founder John D. Rockefeller Sr. kept at least 25% of each of the 34 companies and several controlling interest in.
Today, oil giant ExxonMobil are one of the 34 companies, which members of the Rockefeller Family still own a substantial amount of stock.

David Rockefeller was Class A Director of the **Federal Reserve Bank of New York**

David Rockefeller is a lifelong globalist controlling businesses worldwide. He was invited to attend the inaugural elitist Bilderberg Group meetings, starting with the Holland gathering in 1954. He was a consistent attendee through the decades when he was a member of the "steering committee," which determines the invitation list for the upcoming annual meetings. Invitees have frequently included prominent national figures that have gone on to be elected as political leaders of their respective countries.

David Rockefeller's Prominent Associates
An early connection he developed in the 1950s was with the Central Intelligence Agency (OSS), as well as knowing Allen Dulles and his brother John Foster Dulles; who was an in-law of the family since his college years. It was in Room 3603 in Rockefeller Center that Allen Dulles had set up his OSS, (CIA) WWII operational center after Pearl Harbor, liaising closely with MI6 which also had their principal U.S. operation in the Center. He also knew and associated with the former CIA director Richard Helms, as well as Archibald Roosevelt, Jr., a Chase Bank employee and former CIA agent, whose cousin was the CIA agent, Kermit Roosevelt, Jr., involved in the Iran coup of 1953. Also, in 1953, he had befriended William Bundy, a pivotal CIA analyst for nine years in the 1950s, who became the Agency liaison to the National Security Council, and a subsequent lifelong friend. Moreover, in Cary Reich's biography of his brother Nelson, a former CIA agent states that David was extensively briefed on covert intelligence operations by himself and other Agency division chiefs, under the direction of David's "friend and confidant", CIA Director Allen Dulles,(**who was the organizer and "Director" to Kennedy's Assassination**).

Rockefellers were international bankers, Globalists and part owner of Federal Reserve with close friends and in business with the Bush Family for four generations. They were close friend to CIA Director Allen Dulles...It takes no genius to see the truth...

Senator Prescott Bush
& George W. Bush Sr.

"Everything the Bush Family has, we owe thanks to the Rockefellers." - George W. Bush Sr., 2004

Chapter XVI
America's New Direction Ordered by Those Responsible For President Kennedy's Assassination

No other man has effected the JFK Assassination than the man who killed Lee Harvy Oswald, Jack Ruby. And Jack had some interesting things to say after his arrest that fits the pattern of events that would follow for decades to come.

"But if I am eliminated there won't be any way of knowing. Consequently a whole new form of government is going to take over this country, and I know I won't live to see you another time. My life is in danger here.

(Left picture) A somber, "acting" Lyndon Johnson is sworn into office. (Below picture) Only seconds before, and before TV cameras were turned on, the smiling Johnson and 8F group member & congressman Albert Thomas exchange winks as a sign "mission accomplished."

FBI Director J. Edgar Hoover & President Lyndon B. Johnson

President Johnson and FBI Director J. Edgar Hoover worked well together to cover up the truth behind Kennedy's Assassination. Johnson couldn't have done a better job at appointing Kennedy's enemies to what is regarded as the **fictitious** Warren Commission. Although President Kennedy was the first president in 100 years to order Federal troops into a state to secure the Civil Rights for blacks, and backed programs to help all minorities, Johnson seen it fitting to appoint past KKK Clansman Leader from California, and at the time, Chief Justice of the United States Supreme Court to head an investigation into Kennedy's Assassination. Johnson also appointed Bush Family loyalist and one Kennedy forced out of his decades-long job, past CIA Director Allen Dulles. Prescott Bush and Dick Nixon's close friend Gerald Ford was also appointed by Johnson, and who would come up with "the single bullet miracle theory" along with the now long time Senator Allen Specter. David Rockefeller's eyes to the Assassination, John McCloy was on the Warren Commission. McCloy's job was to make sure everything went smoothly before, during and after the Assassination including in no way the Rockefellers, Bushs or Federal Reserve be connected to the Assassination or the Warren Commission Report.

 Without question, from the day President Kennedy was assassinated, the country was led into another direction that John F. Kennedy wouldn't have allowed it to be led.

As the newly place President from the aftermath of the Globalists, capitalist-elitists and also owners of the Federal Reserve's ordered coup d' etat, Lyndon B. Johnson was quickly sworn into office within in steps of the assassinated President Kennedy's still warm body. As President, Johnson followed orders well either because of his beliefs were the same of those owners of the Federal Reserve responsible for ordering Kennedy's Assassination, or out of fear that he too would fall prey to a short lived presidency.

As not to be an obvious pawn to the Globalists while misleading the public, President Johnson would later sign into law, sent to him by congress, many programs for the poor that the assassinated President Kennedy was backing at the time of his death.

Most importantly to the Globalists owners of the Federal Reserve, Johnson ended the government's distribution of the $2.00 and $5.00 Silver Certificates President Kennedy was using to put the "privately owned" Federal Reserve out of business. He also ordered the destruction of all the $10.00 and $20.00 Silver Certificates being made at the time of Kennedy's Assassination. Johnson's ignoring Kennedy's Executive Order #11110 secured the Federal Reserve's owners of controlling the country's industrial and financial institutions.

"Who ever controls the volume of money in any country, is absolute master of all their industry and commerce."

- Paul Warburg, author of the
Federal Reserve Act

Although it wouldn't be until conspirator and CIA Agent in 1963, George H.W. Bush Sr. would surprisingly get into the White House as vice-president and President Reagan's handler, that Kennedy's Executive Order #11110 would be officially resend and all presidents from Johnson to Reagan ignored Kennedy's Executive Order; most likely out of fear for their own life.

Johnson also signed the "NAFTA type," pro-big business, Republican backed automobile industry's "free trade" treaty with Canada that President Kennedy had refused to sign because he believe it would of cost Americans thousands of jobs and put the United States on a trade road of no return.

As a Senator, Lyndon Johnson for decades directed multi-million dollar projects to Halliburton and Brother Brothers Harriman Companies including Dresser Company; both of which Prescott and son George Bush was stockholders and employees of.

President Johnson also ignored President Kennedy's orders to cut back the amount of troops in Vietnam only to expand the war from only 16,000 advisors in 1963 to 550,000 by 1968 with 1,000 American troops dieing a month.

President Johnson's act was getting old for the Globalists that put him into power…and expensive. The programs for the poor that President Kennedy had planned, that Johnson signed into law, were causing taxes to increase and more importantly, took added money from the war in Vietnam, which cost the Globalists higher profit. President Johnson suddenly and surprisingly announced he would not run for president in 1968. With Johnson out of the way, finally, those Globalists owners of industrial and financial empires would get their Bush-Rockefeller puppet into the White House in Richard M. Nixon…But darkness loomed in the plans of the Globalists to have such a puppet as Richard M. Nixon. As if coming from the past on a white horse, Bobby Kennedy appeared more mature, enlightened and anti-war that in time became a nightmare for those that had murdered his brother, John. Senator Bobby Kennedy, like his brother John, was a breath of fresh air with hope and new ideas. Ending the Vietnam War and expanding social programs were Bobby Kennedy's election primaries battle cry that would get him the Democratic nomination after winning the state of California.

"Some people see things as they are and ask why. I dream of things and ask why not."

Those behind his brother's assassination would have much to worry about. Bobby under his brother's administration as Attorney General and head of the Justice Department was known as a hardhead. Its been said shortly before he won the California Primary, Bobby promised once elected President, he would get to the truth of President John F. Kennedy's Assassination. That alone would have been motive enough to take action against Bobby.

In a hail of gunfire, Bobby Kennedy was assassinated by, to this day, unknown assassins. Evidence has proven beyond question that there was more than one assassin. Finally the

Globalists who also owned the Federal Reserve got their man into the White House...
Richard M. Nixon.

President Nixon stayed loyal to his puppet masters, the Bush & Rockefeller Families, throughout his presidency. He expanded the war by bombing Laos and Cambodia, and no one can for sure know how far Nixon would of expanded the war if given funds from Congress. But Nixon was forced by Congress' funding cuts to find a way of ending America's involvement in Vietnam and Southeast Asia.

Banker & one of the Federal Reserve owners David Rockefeller(left), and (right) Senator Prescott Bush preparing newcomer Dick Nixon for his first campaign.

CIA Agent and son of President Nixon's close friend and political handler, Prescott Bush, George H.W. Bush was appointed Ambassador to the United Nations. In time, Ambassador Bush would convince Nixon to have America side with the People's Republic which was the same Communist branch of government in China that financially backed the United States enemies in Vietnam. In siding with Mao's communists for a seat in the United Nations, America turned its back on ally, the Republic of China and Taiwan.

The United State of America can not be defeated militarily, but will economically from their own greed for individual material self-worth.
- Communist China President Mao Zedong

Under Bush's direction, Nixon opened relations and trading with the Communist People's Republic, which in time Bush Family members invested and made millions of dollars including building China's first golf course and selling them high tech satellites. Once again, the Bush family was back in business with the United States enemy in war;

188

first at Union Bank of New York under Brown Brothers, Harriman Company during World War II they were in business for high profit with Hitler and the Nazis, this time with Communist China who was financially backing North Vietnam.

Prescott Bush Jr.'s company was allowed to sell Communist China communication satellites even though there was an embargo against such sales. The fact his brother, George Bush Sr. was President at the time probably had something to do with it. Prescott Jr. had already built the first golf course in Communist China. Since George Bush Sr. was appointed by family close friend Dick Nixon as ambassador to Communist China, the Bush Family have had a close business relationship with China.

After Vice-President Agnew's resignation, Nixon appointed Gerald Ford vice-president who was a long time friend and campaigner for Nixon and member of the Warren Commission who came up with the factious "single bullet theory" that had sealed the cover up of Kennedy's Assassination in the Warren Commission Report.

President Ford replaced Nixon after he resigned in shame, and to head off impeachment proceedings that would have thrown him out of office. Ford then gave the vice-presidency to long time close friend and business associate to the Bush Family, Nelson Rockefeller. Ford would name George H.W. Bush Sr. as CIA Director, which under Bush's tenure, it is claimed, that over 200 pieces of evidence to President Kennedy's Assassination went missing.

189

The Globalists thought they were back on track to create a new America with a Ford-Rockefeller White House, although their first plan failed to replace Nixon-Agnew with international banker David Rockefeller as president and Ford as VP. But President Ford, already in a tight election race with Jimmy Carter, decided to pardon Richard Nixon shortly before the election from all criminal prosecution and thus upsetting the voters and costing President Ford a defeat.

One would have to wonder if President Ford felt he was in over his head as president and no longer wanted to hold the highest office in America. As a leading member of the Warren Commission, Ford had seen evidence to Kennedy's Assassination and witnessed testimony the public had not heard. Had he figured out the truth of the conspiracy that was orchestrated by David Rockefeller, Allen Dulles, Prescott and George Bush Sr?

It was President Eisenhower in his last speech as president that forewarned the nation of forces that put their own agenda ahead of the welfare of the country.

"We must guard against the acquisition unwarranted influence, whether sought or unsought, by the military industrial complex."
Dwight D. Eisenhower 1961

The public would later find out what President Eisenhower would also say to his brother in May of 1959.

"There is a group of well financed and powerful Texians with influencial friends through out the country and within our government power structure that wish to change America's way of living as we know it. They will do anythting to get their way."

Sen. Prescott Bush and Pres. Eisenhower

190

President Kennedy was on to the powers that wanted to change America.

"The high office of the President has been used to foment a plot to destory America's freedoms and before I leave office, I must inform the citizens of his plight."

- President Kennedy
Was Kennedy speaking of David Rockefeller who had lost so much from Cubian investments and about to lose his hold of the Federal Reserve?

So could of President Ford been onto what was going on from the public's eye? And if so, did he sabotage his own election for the betterment of the country by pardoning Richard Nixon? We may never know the truth, but there is a pattern here with Presidents Eisenhower and Kennedy, then Ford that they knew more of what was going on within the powerful elitist community unknown to the public that they were saying.

Gerald R. Ford, President 1974-1977
The U.S. Justice Dept. in 1974 filed "antitrust" suit against AT&T for having a monopoly. The result was AT&T breaking up in 1982 into seven companies. The competition caused the price of telephone services to go down.

James Earl "Jimmy Carter Jr.
39th President of the United States
From 1977-1981
Carter inheirited many problems
from previous administration.

President Carter inherited a country of people that lacked confidence in their government because of the assassinations of John F. Kennedy, Martin Luther King and Bobby Kennedy, a Warren Commission Report that made no sense, civil unrest over civil rights, the Vietnam War, Watergate and the criminal President Nixon being let off free from his crimes by way of President Ford pardoning him.

191

The Globalists had lost all their power within the White House and would have little to say on how the country would be run. But the Globalists were not going to be denied their profits and began massive layoffs and rising prices during President Carter's years in office. Both unemployment and inflation hit double digits while the economy grew a mere 1 percent, compared to the previous years of three-plus percent growth. Although the media would blame OPEC's rising prices for America's economic problems, in truth, industry and business slow down was caused by those Globalists owning the Federal Reserve. The Globalists, international bankers, had had enough of Carter and did the only thing they knew to get rid of him, aside from another assassination. Their influence raised Federal Reserve's discount rates steadily from 10% in June of 1979 to 21.5% by December of 1980. With such high interest rates, it wasn't any mystery why President Carter was unable to get the economy moving and any chance of re-election died.

Ronald Wilson Reagan
40th President of United States
1981 - 1989

With President Reagan & VP George Bush Sr. the Globalists had their man in the White House in George Bush. George was son of Prescott Bush, who had been a powerful Senator and influential close friend and golfing buddy to President Eisenhower during the 1950s and 60s. Prescott was also within the group of Globalists that included David Rockefeller. The Globalists group, Bilderberg Group included, directed America into a "new world order" of globalism with free trade, cutting taxes to the wealthy and corporations and getting control of populations by indebting them to financial institutions. But the only one obstacle remained to the Globalists total control of American policy, President Reagan.

President Reagan campaigned as a conservative with promises of balancing the Federal Budget which he done as Governor of California, decreasing the Federal Government size and getting the government out of the lives of citizens; not exactly what the Globalists and international bankers had in mind for the country. So to most people within the globalist circle, it wasn't surprising to them to see on the news that the son of Vice-President Bush family friend, one time neighbor and Texas oilman who Bush had save his company from bankruptcy, John Hinckley Sr., attempted to make George Bush president by assassinating President Reagan. But the plan failed when John Hinckley Jr. missed killing President Reagan. But all would not be lost because Reagan was never the same after his near death experience of taking a bullet less than one inch from his heart. Some has said, although Reagan continued to be a great showman during his speeches, as time passed even during his first term, he was becoming ill and increasingly took advice from Vice-President Bush. During Reagan's second term, some White House insiders have said he got so bad that Vice-President Bush was really running the country; just as in future years Vice-President Cheney would make decisions for President G. W. Bush.

President Reagan and Globalist George Bush as his Vice-President marked a time in America's history of drastic change in a "new world order," globalism direction. Some would rather say "not a new direction," but a return to the pre-President Roosevelt days when employers had free reign to run their businesses and treat their employees the way they wanted to and without government or union interference. President Roosevelt's "New Deal" was increasingly ignored while companies were allowed to fire and replace any union or non-union worker going on strike over wages or working conditions.

The pro-business, anti-New Deal policies that began under the Reagan-Bush reign in the White House would continue for at least the next 28 years under the Bush Sr, Clinton and Bush Jr's terms in office. It marked of shift of power and wealth and power within business from a fair profit sharing between employer and employee, to employers having all the power while taking most of the profits as employee's wages stayed the same or at least behind the inflation rate. Benefits also to the employee were cut; including paid vacation, sick days and health insurance.

The American middleclass was under attack by the Globalists while Reagan and Bush put the United States on a worldwide trading path as President Kennedy called it, "of no return." Their free trade policies would cost American workers tens of millions of middleclass jobs over the next 28 years that had fueled a stable and thriving economy for the previous forty years. Tax revenue in the billions were lost from companies outsourcing their manufacturing jobs to Communist China or any country offering cheaper labor for the benefit of the company's higher profits. Soon low level white collar and high tech jobs would be added to company's work outsourcing list.

Their deregulation policies and lack of government oversight allowed Saving & Loans employees to steal millions from their depositors with risky loans to themselves and friends that ended up not being paid back. In total 1,700 Savings & Loans and 1,100 banks went bankrupt during the eight years Reagan was president. Very few people involved in the theft of billions of dollars were punished for their crimes and cost the American taxpayer, at the time, over $125 billion; although the government re-cooped much of the money after they took control of the Savings & Loans until showing a profit.

Corporations were allowed to avoid paying taxes by using their taxable profits to be used to buy their corporate competition as an expense. Some moved their corporate office outside of the United States to avoid paying taxes. Media empires were buying one another to control the one-sided, pro-big business news the public would get. Reagan-Bush's "trickle down economics" failed the middleclass and poor while making fortunes for the wealthy. Their cut taxes to the wealthy and corporations were 100% debt forcing America to barrow so much money that in only eight years, the "give to the wealthy and barrow to pay for it" policy tripled the country's Nation Debt. The Economic Recovery Act of 1981 decreased taxes to the top 1.2% wage earners and corporate earnings making $3.5 million or more from 70% to 50%, which cost the country hundreds of billions of dollars in tax revenue. To the bottom wage earners, income taxes decreased from 14% to 11% while their FICA Tax doubled.

Reagan-Bush's free-wheeling spending fueled the economy to replace and cover up lost Federal Tax revenue from corporations outsourcing millions of manufacturing middleclass jobs. Reagan-Bush came up with a scam to get hundreds of billions of dollars without it showing up on the yearly government's deficit; while being added later to the country's National Debt. They would have one government agency loaning another government agency by taking money out of the citizen's Social Security Fund and deposit it into the government's General Fund. This deceptive "shell game" of moving money from the citizen's Social Security Fund that was collecting interest, and would of been more than enough to sustain an increase of payouts to the "baby boomer generation" that were to begin to retire in January of 2008, into a financial crisis by the early 1990s on how they could keep the ever depleting Social Security Fund solvent once the "baby boomer generation" began to retire. President Reagan's "live for today and don't think about tomorrow" policies would of bankrupted the one-time viable Social Security Fund by 2010 except for congresses intervention in the 1990s to sustain the Fund at least until 2012.

> *The United State of America can not be defeated militarily, but will economically from their own greed for individual material self-worth.*
> - **Communist China President Mao Zedong**

Republicans and the corporate owned media unjustly gave Reagan credit for the fall of the U.S.S.R. while ignoring the truth that Polish Union strikes and the Union movement that spread through Russia, the drain on their treasury from their failing war in Afghanistan and the fact that Communism can't sustain itself economically without a vast exporting business, caused the break up of Communist Russia. The media and republican propaganda machine also ignored, and kept from the public, America's CIA Agency report to the Reagan Administration that it would be only a matter of 7 to 10 years that the U.S.S.R. would fail by way of bankruptcy. But Reagan would not wait out Russia's impending self-destruction from their own financial policies and he continued spending needlessly on building bombs and such failing fantasy projects as "Star Wars" defense systems. Reagan's excuse for spending hundreds of billions on defense that put millions of dollars of profit into the pockets of his past political campaign financial backers was to force Communist Russia to lose the arms race and fail as a country. To this day, the corporate, pro-republican media spreads this false propaganda to the public as if it were written in stone by God Himself.

The Reagan-Bush Administration repealed President Kennedy's Executive Order 11110 that would of put the "privately owner" Federal Reserve out of business. They also repealed the "Fairness in the News Media Doctrine," which gave TV, radio and news print corporations free reign to report, and not report, whatever they wish whether it be one-sided or not without being accountable for its content. This would be the beginning of the end of independent investigative news reports and the complete take over of corporation ownership of what the public would see, hear and read in news.

As of 2000, six corporations own over 90% of all of the news media in the United States; including TV, radio and news print. Also by the mid-1980s, their was a complete change of radio talk show hosts with almost all of the non-conservative talk show hosts being fired and replaced by those pro-corporate, pro-republican, conservative hosts. From 1990 to 2007, 99% talk radio hosts were conservative, pro-republican and pro-corporate.

America began to change like it hadn't for the previous forty years. Reagan-Bush Globalists policies were set in place, which ignored President Roosevelt's "New Deal," anti-trust and anti-monopoly laws. Companies had free reign over hiring and firing employees and breaking up unions. Their policies of free trade, tax cuts for the wealthy and corporations only added debt, living on credit, turning the country and its economy from manufacturing to service, deregulations with little or no oversight from government and almost complete take over by corporations of the news media would slowly head the country towards a 2008 economic meltdown.

 George Herbert Walker Bush
President from:
January 1989 to January 1993

George H.W. Bush Sr.'s final reward for his part in President Kennedy's Assassination and over 26 years of service to his fellow wealthy Globalists was when he became President of the United States. As a past ambassador to United Nation & Communist China who had convinced President Nixon to side with the Communist People's Republic Party led by Mao Zedong over the Republic of China Party in China for a seat into the United Nations, setting up trade agreements with China, Agent & Director of CIA and third generation stockholder of the privately owned United States Federal Reserve, George H.W. Bush continued the "new world order" plan of personal and business associate David Rockefeller. A plan for America that President Eisenhower indirectly forewarned America about in his last speech in office, a plan President Kennedy promised to expose before leaving office and a plan President Kennedy almost stopped with Executive Order #11110, but got him assassinated. A plan assassin to Lee Oswald, Jack Ruby, forewarned Chief Justice to the Supreme Court and then head of the Warren Commission by saying "a new form of government would take over the country; meaning capitalists globalism." A plan that began when the future Federal Reserve owners sent their representatives, in secret, to Jekyll Island in 1910 to create a privately owned central banking system that they would own and thus control "credit & buying power" to all of banking, industry and the population of the United States of America and beyond.

During Bush's years in office, he doubled the National Debt, increased taxes and kept deregulation polices from the Reagan years while corporations outsourced millions of middleclass jobs.

**William Jefferson (Bill) Clinton
President from:
Jan. of 1993 to Jan. of 2001**

From the days after Bill Clinton defeated President George Bush Sr. in November of 1992, well financed right-wing groups used their wealth to smear Clinton's name with endless accusations on anything they could think of in hopes it would stick in the minds of voters. The American media, which over 95% was controlled and owned by only six pro-Globalist, pro-republican corporations, provided a daily platform for those seeking to smear the Clintons. An anonymous letter over the Clintons replacing the White House's travel agents led to an FBI investigation, then to an appointment of "special prosecutor" Kenneth Starr to investigate. The Starr investigation widened to other false accusations and lasted most of President Clinton's two terms in office; costing the taxpayer over $64 million. From investigations that started in May of 1993 and ended in 2000, both President Clinton and Hillary Clinton, were found not to have committed any crimes.

President Clinton's enemies would finally get their scandal on January 17th, 1988. A non-intercourse, 16 month with 9 sexual encounters, between November 15th 1995 and February 28th 1997, affair between Clinton and 22 year old intern Monica Lawinsky was made public. The media and Republicans had a field day with it that lasted until President Clinton left office. After the Republicans were voted in the majority in both houses of Congress, they made the scandal story stayed in the public's eye thanks to the American pro-Republican media. The House of Representatives voted to impeach President Clinton; with only a few Republicans and no Democrats voting for impeachment. In the Senate, the impeachment didn't pass with only Republicans voting for impeachment and both Republicans and all Democrats voting against impeachment. President Clinton left office with the highest approval rating in recent history at 66%.

Much of President Clinton's unending attacks against him were caused by his "pay as we go policy." When Clinton took office, he was saddled with a slumming economy and a previous year's debt from the George Bush Administration of $399 billion. President Clinton during two terms of office, eight years, would reduce the size of the Federal Government, cut taxes to lower income families, make tax cuts available to 90% of all small businesses and increased taxes to the top 1.2% of wealthiest taxpayers and turned record debt from Republican Presidents in the past 12 years to surplus' of over $60 billion and over $120 billion in his last two years. To get to those last two years of surplus years, Clinton battled with a Republican controlled Congress over their demand of a $286 billion tax cut for the wealthiest taxpayers and corporations. Republicans refused to pass a budget and in protest of not getting a tax cut for the wealthy and corporations campaign contributors staged a walk out. Without a budget, all non-essential government business stopped and thousands were sent home from their government jobs. Months later, Republicans returned to work under pressure from voters and passed the budget without tax cuts and what President Clinton wanted in a budget that would cause surplus in the final two years in office.

The first World Trade Center bombing occurred in the basement of one of the towers. Using professional agencies as the New York Police Department, FBI, CIA and international law enforcement agencies, all of those directly involved were arrested and sent to prison. President Clinton also bombed Al Qaeda's camp in Afghanistan and before leaving office forwarded the incoming Bush Administration of Osama Bin Laden's terrorist network and threat to the security of the United States. The Bush Administration ignored President Clinton's forewarnings. Bush and top Security Advisor Rice didn't even open a prepared envelope of top secret information pertaining to the threat Bin Laden and Al Qaeda terrorist were to the United States.

The Clinton years seen prosperity for business and the individual with a boost from the internet going public. President Clinton would sign a NAFTA Trade Treaty which President George Bush Sr's Administration had written and would have signed had Bush Sr. won a second term. Bush also by Executive Order cut. spending in the military drastically which Clinton continued. Clinton signed the "Telecom Act" that allowed corporate owned media to dominate and control the news even more as before. He also signed into law a Welfare Reform bill to cut benefits and increased minimum wages.

 George Walker (G.W.) Bush
President from:
January 2001 to January 2009

Republican President Bush with a Republican controlled Congress marked the first time since 1922 that Republicans controlled all three branches of government. The Capitalists and Globalists could ask for no more. And they weren't let down as the country, guided by Bush Administration , returned to the debt ridden Reagan and Bush Administration's free spending, tax cutting mostly for the wealthy and corporations policies while barrowing to pay for it.

Within two months, the Republican Congress with the President's signature passed an "all pork" bill that spent President Clinton's surpluses of the past two years. Less than six months in office, Bush's $1.35 trillion tax cuts was one of the biggest in America's history; which 85% of tax cuts went to the wealthiest 1.5% and corporations. During

Bush's time as president, the National Debt doubled, exploded to $11.3 trillion dollars. Middleclass household income decreased an average of $1,175 during his first 7 years. During his final year, the stock market dropped, whipped out all gains in the market from the previous seven years. A staggering amount of banks and financial institutions would get themselves into a cash flow crisis; which was caused by a lack of government oversight and the repeal of President Roosevelt's "New Deal" regulations over financial institutions that for over 50 years protected the common investor and depositor from the greed and irresponsible dealings by Wall Street's Financial Institutions.

One of the first things Bush did after taking office was to re-classify Administrative information from the public going back 20 years to include the Reagan-Bush years in the White House. He also requested some in the military to devise plans to invade Iraq.

President G. W. Bush would be highly criticized for his handling the worldwide terrorist threat. In office for seven months, Bush was faced with dealing with 9-11. His Administration, especially Vice-President Dick Cheney, viewed 9-11 as an opportunity to inflame the public by daily parading before TV cameras, radio microphones and gave news print interviews with only one theme in mind, "hate and fear." The Bush Administration's theme worked well in getting the public in a state of "revenge and not justice," as President Clinton's search for justice did after the 1st Trade Center bombing which caught and put in prison for life all those directly connected to it. The Bush White House used the time after 9-11 to ignore the United States Constitution and civil rights of the voters and run the country as they seen fit; including illegal phone taps and reviewing e-mails. Within seven weeks, October 24th 2001, the House of Representatives was presented with the Patriot Act and passed it the next day. After the Senate passed it President Bush signed it the following day. Later it would be revealed that not one congressman read the 900 page Patriot Act before voting for it, nor does anyone know who wrote it; which makes many believe the Patriot Act was sitting around in some right-winger, globalist's desk just waiting for something like 9-11 to happen.

President Bush's policies made tens of millions of dollars for his close friends, the wealthy and corporations. Needlessly invading Afghanistan and Iraq will cost the American taxpayer as much as $3 to $5 trillion after all expenses is counted. Bush-Cheney policies of cutting the amount of Federal regulators gave financial institutions free reign to run their businesses as they saw fit; as it was in the 1920s.

As the Financial Crisis of 2008 began to be made public in October, the Bush Administration did nothing to stop it. While Bear Stearns was having cash flow problems, instead of the Federal Reserve coming to their aid with low interest loans to avoid them from going out of business, JPMorgan Chase Manhattan Bank and other financial institutions from Wall Street announce to the public that they were no longer extending them credit; just as the old timers of the New York Banking Community had done to Knickerbocker Trust Company in 1907. JPMorgan Chase Manhattan Bank, once run by CEO David Rockefeller and a bank the Rockefeller Family continue to own a substantial amount of stock in, as well as the privately owner of the Federal Reserve, bought Bear Stearns for pennies on the dollar after receiving a low interest loan in the tens of billions of dollars from the Federal Reserve. Shortly thereafter Secretary of the United States Treasury, Henry Paulson, scared taxpayers into pressuring Congress to pass a $700 billion "bailout" bill to pay for Wall Street's irresponsible Financial Institutions policies. Paulson & Bush used fear by threatening them the "If he didn't get the money very soon, depositors would be unable to get their money out of ATM machine." Even before Paulson and Bush chose to use such words, they knew every depositor's account was insured by the United States Government up to $100,000. But their threats worked and the bill finally got passed without restrictions. But the results of his threats caused a "panic" among many depositors, who the next day, withdrew their money and the Financial Crisis ballooned to epidemic size. In the next three weeks, for one example, depositors from Washington Mutual on the west coast withdrew over $18 billion which put such a stress on the Bank's cash flow, they filed bankruptcy. And once again, the Federal Reserve did nothing while JPMorgan Chase Manhattan Bank bought them for pennies on the dollar; which was also convenient to JPMorgan Chase Manhattan Bank since for the past two years they had been looking to expand their east coast business to the west coast.

Besides the Federal Reserve all but standing by and doing little to prevent Bear Stearns and Washington Mutual Banking from going bankrupt and sold for pennies on the dollar to New York's JPMorgan Chase Manhattan Bank, President Bush and the Federal Reserve did nothing to end the collapse of the New York Stock Market. Had Bush suspended the capital gains tax cuts, or enacted a new capital gains tax on stocks to 40% or 50%, it would have stopped the panic selling by stock holders before the Stock Market lost trillions of dollars.

President Bush would leave office in January of 2009 as being the lowest rated and least popular president since Republican President Hoover left office in 1929. But more importantly to Bush, the wealthy got richer during his terms in the White House.

George Herbert Walker Bush Jr. was born into a wealthy family, lived through out his life with the family's wealth backing him and paying for his many mistakes on his way to becoming president. His family and "have more" family friends can be sure grateful for how he took good care of them while in office with tax cuts, no bid contracts and two needless wars that made them much more wealthier than they were when he took office.

Bush's policies followed the policies of his father George Bush, Clinton and Reagan, who must also take blame for the financial Worldwide Crisis of 2008 and the terrible condition the country would be in as President Obama takes office in 2009.

State of the United States of America

Since the time representatives of the world's most powerful international bankers met in secret on Jekyll Island in 1913, their bosses goal was first to gain control of the largest pool of money in the world, the United States Currency.

Vanderlip wrote in his 1935 autobiography "From Farmboy to Financier".
(Pertaining to the Jekyll Island meeting.)

"I was as secretive, indeed I was as furtive as any conspirator. Discovery, we knew, simply must not happen, or else all our time and effort would have been wasted. If it were to be exposed that our particular group had got together and written a banking bill, that bill would have no chance whatever of passage by Congress...I do not feel it is any exaggeration, (overstate) to speak of our expedition to Jekyll Island as the occasion of the actual conception of what eventually became the Federal Reserve System."

Frank Vanderlip
President to:
National City Bank
of New York

Once they owned the Federal Reserve, they became masters to all of the country's banking, industry and politicians as well as having influence worldwide.

"Who ever controls the volume of money in any country, is absolute master of all their industry and commerce."

- Paul Warburg, author of the Federal Reserve Act

America's laws became meaningless to them, once they got control of its currency.

"Give me the power to issue a nation's money, and I care not who writes the laws."

- Amschel Rothschild, founder of Rothschild Banking Empire

Politicians were elected into office; but it would be the Federal Reserve owners that would control the money supply to financial institutions that made loans to businesses and individuals; thus controlling the economy and the future of elected politicians.

"When the President signs this bill,
(meaning the Federal Reserve Act that gave 12 people control and ownership of United States currency.)
the invisible government of the monetary power will be legalized... The worst legislation crime of the ages is perpetrated by this banking and currency bill." - Charles A. Lindbergh Sr., 1913

Few people would have the courage to challenge the Globalists authority to own the Federal Reserve and control the United States currency.

Pres. Franklin D. Roosevelt * Congressman McFadden * Pres. John F. Kennedy

Roosevelt before taking office questioned the Globalists authority to own the Federal Reserve and blamed their irresponsible handling of the taxpayers money for getting the United States into the Great Depression; which led to an assassination attempt on his life conspired by the Globalists. Then once he became President, the Globalists attempted to over thrown him from office, called the Business Plot. **Congressman McFadden** in 1933 filed charges against those running and owning the Federal Reserve for fraud, corruption and irresponsible handling of the taxpayer's money for their own gain, then only days after there were two assassination attempts on his life. **President Kennedy** was assassinated for Executive Order #11110 that put out Silver Certificates to compete with the Federal Reserve Notes that in six years would of put the Federal Reserve out of business, eliminate the country's National Debt and no longer would the Globalist be able to control and use the largest pool of money in the world as their own personal bank account to receive huge loans for their own financial empire.

Before the Reagan-Bush presidency took over with their reign of destroying the middleclass with "trickle down economics" policies and deregulating business restrictions, which for over three decades protected the average citizen from big business greed, American's way of life from 1948 to 1980 was the most prosperous in United

States history. America in 1980 was the greatest credited country of in history of the world. But in less than 25 years of pro-corporate, deregulation and Republican policies the United States in 2006 became the most indebted country in the history of the world. America went from manufacturing more goods than any country on the planet to importing more goods than any country, which caused the largest trade deficit on earth and a collapsing dollar. In 27 years, 16% of all wages earned in the United State went from the poor and middleclass to the top 1% of wage earners. As was the case in the mid-1920s, today's top wage earners make almost 25% of all wages in the United States; unlike in 1980 the top 1% of wage earners took only 8% of all wages made.

President Kennedy fought such pro-big business, globalism policies the Reagan, Bush, Clinton and Bush Jr. Presidencies promoted. Had John F. Kennedy and Robert Kennedy not been assassinated by the very people wanting such pro-big business, globalism policies, America's way of life would have continued to prosper instead of being taken over by corporate idealism, seductive materialism, individualism and globalism that has benefited the wealthy few.

In 2008, as Joe Kennedy did in 1928, most of those in the know on Wall Street, also knew of a Financial Crisis and Stock Market collapse in the near future. And as Joe Kennedy did in 1928, most of those on Wall Street, sold their stock in early 2008. No matter what you've read of Joe Kennedy, the facts remain that he was an expert in economics and in his time the youngest bank president in the United States at Columbia Banking. Joe learned from history when to get in the stock market and when to get out!

John, Bobby and Ted Kennedy were or are not saints, but they as all the Kennedys were taught, "By their wealth it is their duty to give back," as they have. History tells us, Joe Kennedy sided with the common taxpayer when he as Chairman of the Security & Exchange Commission wrote many of the financial regulations into law that protected the investor from corporate unending greed. President John Kennedy sided with the civil rights leaders, signed Women's Equal Pay Act and refused to sign the Automobile Parts Free Trade Agreement because it would cost Americans their jobs.

And for that alone, we must keep his memory alive!

President Johnson ignored President Kennedy's Executive Order 11110.

President Lyndon Johnson issued a proclamation on June 24, 1968, that all Federal Reserve Silver Certificates were merely *fiat* legal tender and could not be redeemed in silver.

To the reader

*Thank you for taking out your time to read **Powers Behind JFK Assassination.** I hope you now not only have a much better understanding to the events and cover up of President John F. Kennedy's Assassination, but of the American Banking System and it's history, as well as American history pertaining to characters and events which the book covered.*
Sincerely, Randolph Jason Polasek

To order more copies of
Powers Behind JFK Assassination
go to: www.powersbehindjfkassassination.com
or e-mail me at: randolphpolasek@yahoo.com
with subject: Powers Behind JFK Assassination